PENGUIN BOOKS

BIRTH OVER THIRTY-FIVE

Sheila Kitzinger, an internationally respected educator and writer on birth and motherhood, brings to her writing a unique ability to translate academic research findings into the kind of practical information women can apply to themselves and to their lives.

Born in England and educated as a social anthropologist at Oxford, she has taught at the University of Edinburgh and done field research on sex, pregnancy, and childbirth among women in settings as diverse as Jamaica, Japan, Mexico, the former USSR, and among the Maori of New Zealand. She lectures widely in North and South America, Australia, in Western Europe, in Eastern European countries, and in Great Britain. In addition to this title, Penguin also publishes *The Experience of Childbirth*, *The Experience of Breastfeeding*, and *Woman's Experience of Sex*. The mother of five daughters, Sheila Kitzinger lives near Oxford, in England.

BIRTH over
THIRTY-FIVE

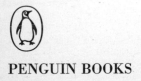

Sheila Kitzinger

EDITED FOR THE UNITED STATES BY
PENNY SIMKIN, R.P.T.

Illustrations by Jo Nesbitt

PENGUIN BOOKS

PENGUIN BOOKS
Published by the Penguin Group
Penguin Books USA Inc., 375 Hudson Street, New York, New York 10014, U.S.A.
Penguin Books Ltd, 27 Wrights Lane, London W8 5TZ, England
Penguin Books Australia Ltd, Ringwood, Victoria, Australia
Penguin Books Canada Ltd, 10 Alcorn Avenue,
Toronto, Ontario, Canada M4V 3B2
Penguin Books (N.Z.) Ltd, 182–190 Wairau Road, Auckland 10, New Zealand

Penguin Books Ltd, Registered Offices:
Harmondsworth, Middlesex, England

Birth Over Thirty first published in Great Britain by Sheldon Press 1982
Revised edition published in the United States of America in Penguin Books 1985
This expanded and updated edition entitled *Birth Over Thirty-Five* published by
Sheldon Press 1994
Published in Penguin Books 1995

10 9 8 7 6 5 4 3 2 1

A NOTE TO THE READER
The ideas, procedures, and suggestions contained in this book are not intended as
a substitute for consulting with your physician. All matters regarding your health
require medical supervision.

Grateful acknowledgment is made to Olwyn Hughes Literary Agency for permission
to reprint six lines from "Three Women" by Sylvia Plath from *Winter Trees*, copy-
right © Ted Hughes, 1971, 1972, published by Faber and Faber, London, and
Harper & Row, New York; and to Professor Gordon Stirrat and Grant McIntyre Ltd.
for permission to quote from *Obstetrics*.

LIBRARY OF CONGRESS CATALOGING IN PUBLICATION DATA
Kitzinger, Sheila.
Birth over thirty-five / Sheila Kitzinger ; edited for the United
States by Penny Simkin ; illustrated by Jo Nesbitt.
p. cm.
Originally published: New York, NY : Penguin Books, 1985.
Includes bibliographical references and index.
ISBN 0 14 02.4141 8
1. Pregnancy in middle age.   2. Childbirth in middle age.
I. Simkin, Penny, 1938–   . II. Title.
RG556.6.K56   1995
618.2—dc20   94-21963

Printed in the United States of America
Set in Bodoni Book
Designed by Kathryn Parise

Contents

This is not a how-to-book

Introduction

More and more women are deciding to have a baby when they are in their thirties or early forties. Five percent of births are to women in this age group—twice the figure of the mid-1970s. Yet most books written for expectant mothers imply that they are younger, do not give the specific information an older mother wants, and fail to explore the often complex emotional aspects of birth for a woman who is not merely outside the safest age range in which to have a baby, but who may have a successful career behind her and be in the full activity of creative and rewarding work outside the home.

This is not a how-to book, packed with dos and don'ts. It is based on women's actual experiences and a wide variety of different responses to similar challenges. I am very grateful to all those who wrote about their experiences and have learned a great deal from them. Some of these were people who have been in my own childbirth classes, and I was able to talk with them at length and knew them well. The greatest proportion consisted of 289 women who got in touch following a note in a British national newspaper asking for help. Women in South Africa also wrote following an article in *The Johannesburg Star*, and material from twenty-eight of their letters is included. Women wrote lengthy accounts, often in astonishing detail, and were very open and honest about their negative as well as their positive reactions to the pregnancy, the baby, and the changes that come after the birth.

The gusto with which they wrote was expressed by one woman who, in the middle of her account, suddenly exclaimed: "God, I'm so enjoying writing all this down! It's like a confessional!" As I studied the material, I was struck with admiration for women's courage, their capacity for giving, and their strength. Many of the letters were very moving. Some were hilariously funny. The most striking thing was the generous way in which they all shared what they knew. I felt part of a great sisterhood! Sometimes there was a father's account, too, or a message from older children, or from daughters who were themselves late-born children, and these were a bonus.

I have had two children myself while in my thirties, the fourth and fifth in a family of five. But in the book I have concentrated on those aspects of childbirth and parenthood that women themselves talked about most often, rather than approaching it from personal preconceptions concerning what was important. The synopsis with which I started was quite different from the material that eventually emerged.

I have not attempted to include in this book anything about how to prepare for labor. I hope that all older mothers will seek out good childbirth classes, and they may find my books helpful: *Pregnancy Day by Day, The Experience of Childbirth*, and *Giving Birth, How It Really Feels*. Nor is there any discussion of how to choose where to have the baby. That information is in *Homebirth and Other Alternatives to Hospital*, and *Your Baby; Your Way*. Help with the practical and psychological aspects of breastfeeding can be found in *The Experience of Breastfeeding* and *Breastfeeding Your Baby*. I hope, however, to have written in a way that will mean that the woman over thirty-five, especially one having her first baby, and any woman having another baby after a gap, will feel she understands what is happening to her, knows how to take an active part in her pregnancy and birth, and gains in confidence to cope with the challenges before and after the baby comes.

SHEILA KITZINGER
Standlake Manor,
Near Witney,
Oxfordshire

BIRTH over THIRTY-FIVE

1 &

Deciding to Have a Baby

Thirty . . . forty . . . fifty . . . these birthdays are usually thought of as watersheds in a woman's life, a time for personal stocktaking, but also one full of inherent warnings of failing powers. Before the birthday, she has potential. After it, she is supposed to be past her best and begins to age rapidly. The cosmetics industry, exploiting self-doubts and fears, urges us to buy special "youth dew" and the cream for the "mature" skin with the miracle ingredient guaranteed to plump out degenerating cells.

It is not only that women may look in their mirrors more anxiously for the lines of laughter and experience, but this is a time when they often ask, "Who am I really?," "What am I doing with my life?," "Is this what I want?," and "Where do I go from here?"

The upshot of all this is that more and more women in their late thirties and forties are deciding that they will have a baby, either a first baby or another one "before it is too late," before the biological clock stops ticking.

For others, however, it is part of a long-term plan and what they have always intended. Some expect to have a career and *then* babies. Though it is often believed that women having late babies must be career women who cannot make space for a baby in their

busy lives, research shows that only about 5 percent put off motherhood for career reasons. Some women want babies from early on
but discover that circumstances are against them. Claire says she
would have had a baby before but could not find the right man
and did not contemplate being a single mother. The likely fathers
were all "unstable divorcés" who changed their minds when it
came to marriage, "leaving me feeling deserted." She did get pregnant "ineptly" by "an immature mature postgraduate," but he did
not like the idea of marriage either, so she went through "the
traumatic but fascinating experience of an abortion." When she
met a "steady, reliable guy" a year later they married as soon as
possible and she became triumphantly, if belatedly, pregnant at
thirty-eight.

A late pregnancy may be for very personal reasons because a
woman did not feel "ready" before. As one put it:

> I wasn't mature enough to risk having a baby. I needed my work
> to lose my self-centeredness and be aware of other people's prob-
> lems. If I'd had a baby earlier I'd have been fighting for my own
> rights.

Another delayed having a baby because everything she had read
about motherhood painted a pretty depressing picture, particularly
of "nonworking" mothers. "My work was my life for fifteen years.
If I had given it up earlier I know I could have resented the baby."
Some women embarking on a late pregnancy see it, even then, as,
in one woman's words, "a hole in my career for a few years."

Some couples have hoped for a baby for a long time but only
get down to doing anything about seeking medical help or starting
the more complicated investigations and operations as a birthday
crisis looms.

The Single Mother

Over-thirty-fives are often in a second marriage or committed relationship. They may each have had children with a former partner, too. A man—especially one in his fifties—sometimes feels that he has "done all that" and is surprised when the woman says she would like a baby. But other older men are delighted to start out on this fresh phase of their lives with the expectation of a new family. Whatever the situation, this is a subject a couple need to discuss openly, with its implications in terms of the stresses and benefits of relationships with other children, their own relationship, the financial consequences, and the extra work that a baby entails—and how it can be shared between them. There are probably no crystal-clear answers to the questions raised, but communicating about such matters from the start makes it much easier to cope with the inevitable challenges of parenthood, and to confront them *together*.

Increasing numbers of women having babies over thirty-five are not married. Margaret had been frightened of marriage for a long time. She had lived with a man who was violent and destructive and beat her up. When that affair finished, there followed a period in which she could not trust men at all. But then, she said, she realized she was getting "a bit empty inside; all those years of periods and no children." She met a beautiful stranger, did not even know his last name until some months later, and could not speak his language, but knew that she passionately wanted his child. It was partly, she thinks, because she had had to take care of elderly parents and their farm for many years and partly because of an inherited guilt about enjoying life, that it had all been so delayed. It was a "one-night stand. In *Tess of the d'Urbervilles*, Thomas Hardy says that the time for loving and the man to love do not often come at the same time. But for me they did," she says. She conceived that night.

"I don't seem to have a talent for long-term and fulfilling relationships with men," Jane, a writer, explained, "but I don't see why, since I have the great good fortune to be in a position to support my own children, this should stop me being a mother." So she had a very brief encounter with a man while vacationing on a Mediterranean island. Even so, when she discovered she was pregnant she was "absolutely terrified" and says her mind was "whirling around like a rat in a trap, moments of heart-stopping terror, and yet these flashes of sheer delight." Another woman, in a lesbian relationship, says she felt very alone when she saw friends with their children. She was delighted to become pregnant following artificial insemination, and "now I'm one of the crowd!"

There are women living together, too, perhaps in a lesbian partnership, perhaps in a women's commune, who are likely to delay pregnancy until they feel sure this is the right thing to do, and that there is enough stability in their relationships for it to be the right time to do it. For these, a network of loving women, rather than conventional marriage, offers a basis for embarking on the adventure of bearing and bringing up a child. Some women believe that this may be both a safer and saner environment for a child than one in which male values predominate.

A number of women over thirty-five who have written to me about why they got pregnant say they did so because they or their partners were unemployed or laid off—yet one more alarming effect of an economic crisis, with long-term consequences!

"Surprise" Babies

Some women conceiving at this age are having "surprise" babies, either totally or half accidentally. A woman concludes, for example, that she has been on the pill long enough, or that she should no longer be on it when over thirty-five, and that it would be safer for her health to use some other method of contraception, and discovers that alternatives are not so reliable. Or she comes off the pill because of its side effects and decides to "take a chance." Christine stopped the pill because of "debilitating headaches":

When I eventually realized I was pregnant, no one could have been more surprised than I. My husband was shocked, too, and I felt I had placed a burden on our relationship which took almost five months to untangle. I was terrified at what I had done, but as it was totally my responsibility I came to accept it.

Although she felt guilty about the pregnancy, it does take two to make a baby, and maybe her husband should have been more concerned about her headaches and considered a vasectomy. It is, anyway, a classic case of failure of communication between a couple. At least the crisis got them talking to each other again.

Another woman stopped the pill, had amenorrhea (her periods stopped), and was being investigated for infertility:

I didn't know I was pregnant until I felt the baby move. At first I thought I had indigestion and had been worrying about putting on weight.

This woman is a doctor. She wanted a baby, but realizing she was pregnant came as a great shock.

A Catholic who believes it is wrong to use any form of birth control except the "rhythm method," which she dismisses as "a joke," thought it impossible to conceive because her husband had had an operation as a result of which he was told by the surgeons he could not father children. With five children already and very short of money, she felt the pregnancy was a "disaster," and she also felt acutely embarrassed to be pregnant again in her mid-forties. But she gradually came to accept "the awful fact," and later, far from hiding the baby in her carriage in the yard, as she thought she would, she "pranced around the town showing her off."

Jane, age thirty-nine, had taken a year's leave of absence to finish what she calls "a boring academic book" when she discovered she was pregnant. Her first reaction was one of panic, but when she thought about it she says that something in her was "amazed and glad." She was already sharing the house with a close woman friend who was excited by the news and willing to share child care with her. Having made these arrangements, her pregnancy was "a long, dreamy, and tranquil time." She felt not only special, but blessed, and she describes it as the "Saint Elizabeth syndrome," although other people were telling her that she must be crazy and her own mother was "shocked and upset," accusing her of irresponsibility. She found the whole experience of pregnancy and childbirth, even a very painful and difficult labor, a deeply satisfying one.

Decisions, Decisions

Even when conception is an accident, the decision to go ahead with the pregnancy is usually a conscious and carefully thought out one, and there is no mistake about that. Women often feel under pressure all the same and, like Christine, are submerged under waves of guilt. One woman said she was under open pressure from her anxious psychiatrist advising her to have an abortion when she became pregnant during a serious depressive illness. She found this terribly upsetting, partly because she was feeling very pleased with herself for the first time in years. She continued with the pregnancy, feeling guilty but "secretly rather smug" and "one up" on the psychiatrist. By the time the baby was five months old, she no longer needed a psychiatrist.

Feeling guilty can mean that a pregnancy continues because the alternative seems too awful. Harriet, age forty, went to the hospital to have an abortion, where the nurse preparing her for the operation said, "Oh dear, Doctor won't like *this!*" Harriet got up and left. Whatever the doctor thought, it was she who was having the baby and who was committed to bringing up the child afterward. Pressures can also be exerted the other way and a late pregnancy be made to sound like an ominous and nasty illness, bearing such great risks of having an abnormal baby that a woman feels she cannot go through with it for this reason alone.

The single mother may have special qualms about the decision she has made. One said that all through pregnancy she kept wondering whether she was doing the right thing in planning to keep the baby, but felt sure she wanted the child with a more consistent longing than she ever had for a man.

Occasionally a pregnancy catches the woman in her forties so caught up in her own busy life that, thinking she is beginning menopause, she does not find out she is pregnant until it is too late for an abortion. This happened in a distressing way with Elizabeth, after a brief temporary reconciliation with her former husband when she was recovering from alcoholism. One day she felt flickering movements in her abdomen, and it dawned on her with horror that she was pregnant. She felt she owed it to the baby to give her up for adoption, but found it very difficult in the home for unmarried mothers, where most of the women, who were all much younger, intended to keep their babies. One girl told her, "You treat it like it was throwing away dirt."

But most women having babies at this age do so because this is what they want. And even if the decision is one that follows on the fact of conception, the realization brings not only shock and some apprehension, but also a delighted surprise and bubbling, if submerged, excitement.

There are also, of course, second marriages, second "chances" in life, bringing with them second, or sometimes first, families, or at least "one for him." With any woman who already has grown-up or school-age children, the decision making is mixed with anxiety about how the older ones will cope. Will they see it as a loss of love? Can they handle the experience of having new family members younger than they as well as a new proxy father? What effect will a baby sibling have on adolescents who are still very uncertain of their own sexuality and their own identity? Perhaps they will never come home; perhaps they will feel that mother is somehow competing with them; perhaps they will feel rejected and unwanted.

Some of those who have babies at this age have been happy and confident in their careers and only feel able to go ahead and have a baby when they feel satisfied they have achieved something in their working lives. Motherhood then comes as a welcome fresh start and something else in which they hope they can also use their skills.

One woman who wrote had already decided on sterilization. Her lover mentioned having children, but she says she ignored this and assumed the remarks "were just sentimental indulgences brought on by a new relationship." Arrangements for the operation were delayed because she was going on vacation and then she had a conference to attend. During this time she began to feel that having a baby with this particular partner would be "a shared affair, and not me as a female founding a dynasty for some man." She went ahead and had a child, though the couple do not live together and do not intend to in the future. The plan is for the baby to be in her mother's home for the first two months, with her father there for most of the time, too, and then for the baby to move to the father's apartment.

New Responsibilities

For some women it comes as a shock that the confidence they felt in teaching or running a business, for example, wanes when they are faced with the responsibilities of caring for a baby and they have to come to terms with themselves in a new way.

Delia, age forty-two, had been a very capable social worker accustomed to dealing with "confused adolescents, distressed mothers, and old people." She was amazed at her vulnerability and the swing of her constantly changing emotions in the hospital after having the baby: "How *could* I have let them boss me around like that? And why did I get so worked up about the different advice coming from everybody under the sun?" And when she went on feeling utterly incompetent and dogged with anxiety throughout the first year after the baby's arrival, she realized that she was suffering from chronic depression. She needed to talk about it and to be able to get on the telephone to someone supportive when she felt most isolated. When she was able to do this, she worked through the experience and believed that she had learned something about herself. She is not the invincible, all-giving person as whom she had masqueraded. There are times when she needs to *take* as well as to give, and she can now relax and receive from other people as well.

Other women start out on motherhood at this age largely because they feel they have never succeeded completely at anything else and hope that this is something they can do at last. Although it might seem they would be doomed to failure and that it is one of the worst reasons for having a baby, nearly all those who have described to me this emotional journey feel they have discovered themselves and have attained a new maturity and security. Perhaps when they began to trust themselves and had the courage to make decisions based on their own experience of life, the step was already taken, and the pregnancy confirmed this rather than being the cause of it.

Sue, for example, said she was a "failed academic." She had always felt slightly apologetic about her job as a nursery school teacher with her first partner, himself an academic. They were unhappy together and the relationship broke up. Six years later, she started a relationship with Dan, another academic. She gave up work outside the home when they had a baby, and, in spite of feeling diminished in status by being "only a mother" when with feminist friends who have put mothering gladly behind them or never taken it on, admits that having a baby "releases" her to "do nothing with justification," something she has always wanted to do but has never had the confidence to admit. One of the most important things for Sue is that she is not alone in caring for the baby, as if it is a task only she could do and for which innate "maternal instincts" are sufficient. Dan shares in everything, including the night work, and is almost as involved as she is herself. Because he does not feel it is second-class work, she is not put on the defensive about her role as a mother.

Reason to Conceive

Some babies are conceived nowadays because the woman wants satisfying work outside the home and, in the present economic situation, cannot get it. Frustrated and feeling the need for a job that meets her abilities, she opts for a baby almost as a second-best choice. This may work in the early days, but once the child is at school she is faced with the problem again. There are added financial responsibilities, and she has renewed ties at home. The baby has allowed her to bridge a difficult time, but the same difficulty reasserts itself.

One reason why a couple may put off having a baby is that one or the other partner, or both, have come from an unhappy family and do not want to perpetuate this misery. One woman told me, for example, "My own family has given me a poor pattern of personal relationships, and I felt trapped in my parents' failure." This emotional background can mean that neither partner is certain about whether it is right to have a baby at all. One partner usually gains in confidence through the other's love over the years, and the sense that now is the time to start out on the adventure of parenthood together grows out of the feeling of satisfaction in the couple's relationship. Without it, neither may ever feel ready for a child. Janet delayed till she was nearly forty for this reason but is now "hooked" on having babies. "I am," she said, "like a convert to a new religion!"

Some women admit they had a baby, or another baby, for selfish reasons. "If I had heard anyone else give this reason," Geraldine confessed, "I would have thought they were mad. It was quite irrational. I was very depressed, hated the house we live in, resented doing anything to it or buying anything for it." Her three children were at school and her husband immersed in his civil-service career, caught up in "the rat race." "I wanted to tie myself down to the family again. I knew I was drifting away and thought I could recapture some of the happiness we had earlier in our marriage."

Babies cannot really be used to patch up a failing relationship, or, at least, if they are conceived in this hope, other things have to happen between the couple before any fresh start can take place. Fortunately, Geraldine and David both responded to the challenge, and after a frightening first year or so following the birth, when she was depressed and felt she was living under a permanent black cloud, they talked things through as they never had before and made radical adjustments in their life together. He gave up his job, which was a demanding one and meant that he really saw the children only on weekends, and took another that allowed Geraldine to get a postgraduate degree and him to look after the family for one day a week, as well as share much more in caring for all four generally. She at last feels like a person again and says she has learned "It is too easy to become a passive dependent." She had believed herself indispensable in this passive role but now realizes that "there's nothing I do for my children that they cannot either do for themselves or that someone else can do for them." This is "liberating knowledge" and gives her freedom to enjoy them as people, rather than objects to be serviced. The stress of having a baby in an unhappy relationship can be used constructively to push the couple out of a rut, but they have to be able to make use of the experience and to *create* change, not just let things happen to them.

New Dependency

For a woman who has been busily occupied with her career, however, pregnancy brings with it a new dependency in which she may luxuriate and enjoy the sense of being cherished. Sally had a demanding job in public relations and says that children were just "things that happened to friends." Her first marriage broke up and she remarried and started a family at thirty-five: "I loved being treated in a special way by everyone." This feeling of being valued has continued after the births of her two children largely because her husband is a "sharing, caring partner in all things." For other women the sense of worth gained by the pregnancy is destroyed when caring for a new baby in social isolation. They feel drained of strength, and of their selfhood.

Another woman who welcomed being "taken over" by a process she trusted completely said she had had "a great time" in her professional career, "twenty years of freedom to plan my own life and spend time on what appealed to me," and now pregnancy and birth brought for the first time "something taken out of my hands . . . to use me." She enjoyed being in touch with her feelings in a new way, with the sense that life was expressing itself *through* her, while she learned the flexibility to respond to its demands.

Many women say that pregnancy also brings a sense of oneness with creation, even though they may never have thought of themselves as religious or mystical. The feeling of nurturing another life, of being part of a universal tradition, was how one woman described her exultation in pregnancy.

Being with child also changes other people's ideas of you. "Male colleagues at work," one woman says, "seem to see me in a different role. (Perhaps I'm not so threatening now!) They beam at me all the time with stars in their eyes and talk about their children." She enjoyed seeing this different reflection of self in those with whom she was in constant contact.

We do not usually put such pleasures into words, and perhaps they sound minor when we do, but for anyone, a woman or a man, who has been scurrying around issuing documents and mailing pieces of paper to other people who are engrossed in the same activities, life when a baby is on the way and as a parent takes on a completely new meaning.

This is what happened for Shelley, who had been a cabaret dancer and then an airline attendant. When she married a man much older than herself, she had her IUD taken out and conceived immediately. There had been no time to think about the effects on their relationship or why she was trying to get pregnant. But looking back at it now she says:

Without a doubt if Josh had not come we would have been divorced. To me our marriage would have been like a long date

and I would have dumped him as I had many previous boy-
friends. What a blessing I hung in there because now I realize
what a wonderful soul mate I have, and my happiness often
frightens me.

There is another passive acceptance of pregnancy, however, that
has a more negative aspect. This is the mental state in which a
woman considers termination because she really does not want the
child but cannot face the abortion. Ann said she was frightened
and deeply shocked when she learned she was pregnant at forty-
one. She went to get an abortion but was too confused and uncertain to go through with the operation. For several weeks afterward,
she refused to acknowledge that she was pregnant, but "when I
had to accept it I was plunged into deep depression, sitting for
long periods in a large armchair like a hamster in a nest." The
inner anger she felt continued throughout the pregnancy, but once
she started to see her doctor and it was clear that someone else
obviously cared about the baby, she began to feel she could cope.
In a way, she handed over her emotional link with the baby. Fortunately she and her husband could afford day care and she was
soon back at work. Now fifty-five, she says, "My husband delights
in her. As for me—well, I love her but at times I wish there was
no child at home." It sounds as if both Ann and her daughter are
missing out. But perhaps there was no other way.

After Abortions

An older woman may have had previous abortions, and sometimes
this means that her pregnancy is fraught with anxiety which she
may find it difficult to acknowledge. She may be afraid that she
has damaged her body, or that in some way she will be punished
for getting rid of an unwanted baby. For many—probably most—
women, abortion is not an easy decision, and it casts a long shadow
on the future.

In the first weeks of pregnancy a woman may relive some of the strong emotions experienced with a previous terminated pregnancy. As the months pass, she may wonder what that baby would have been like, and grieve over it. The relief felt after having a successful abortion often obliterates any awareness that a woman may need to mourn her loss as well. Grieving is repressed or delayed —sometimes to emerge only much later when she is pregnant with a much-wanted baby.

A Painful Longing

A woman may come off the pill when she has been on it for many years, or give up her job intending to settle down to a pregnancy at last, only to discover that she is subfertile and that it is difficult to start a pregnancy, or to hold on to one that has started. Ova may be less likely to ripen. After all, they have been stored inside a baby girl's ovaries since birth. They may not be released regularly as a woman approaches menopause. Her uterus may not have the nutrients that the developing cell cluster needs in order to be implanted. There is a gradual and natural decline in fertility from the age of twenty-eight until thirty-five, after which the drop is steeper. When a woman is twenty-three her chances of having a baby are around 95 percent. As she approaches forty, this has dropped to 75 percent. There is a difference, however, if she is in a new sexual relationship, if only because she is likely to be having intercourse more often. Then her chances of success shoot up! With artificial insemination, it has been found that when a woman is just past thirty-five, six out of ten implantations are successful, at least in terms of enabling an embryo to develop for more than six weeks. Once she is over forty, it is down to five out of ten.

Artificial Conception

One line of treatment often entails artificial conception—starting a pregnancy outside your body. Once fertilization has been achieved, the developing cell cluster is introduced into your uterus in the hope that it will become implanted and grow. This may entail using your own or donor eggs and your partner's or donor sperm, and any combination of these. For many women fertility treatment brings no miracle. Doctors are not always honest about their failures, preferring to emphasize successes, and clinics sometimes present misleading statistics concerning success rates.

Even when fertility treatment is successful, it may take a very long time, with raised hopes followed by despair, over months, and sometimes years. Each failed attempt can make a woman feel more depressed. The hope of conception is likely to become the center around which your life has to revolve. You may feel emotionally drained. Sex is fraught with anxiety—no longer spontaneous or joyful. The struggle to conceive destroys the sense of intimacy you feel about your body and your relationship with your partner. You get to be dependent on doctors and technicians.

There are medical risks with infertility treatment, too. Drugs to produce superovulation often have side effects and may cause sickness. Following successful superovulation and implantation you may be told that you are pregnant with three or more babies. Because there are often medical problems in multiple pregnancies, and because the babies are likely to be premature and frail, you may be advised to have "selective reduction"—abortion—to reduce the number to two, in itself a distressing experience.

The longing to carry and give birth to a child must be weighed against the personal stress that fertility treatment may entail, the cost of prolonged treatment, and the possibility of failure. You cannot make a once-and-for-all decision about this. If you start on fertility treatment, you need to assess and reassess your priorities all along the way.

Older women may face other problems, too. They are more likely to have uterine fibroids (lumps), which, though not dangerous, make pregnancy less likely, and blocked fallopian tubes, which result from infection and scarring, so that the cell cluster cannot travel along the tubes to the uterus. Women over thirty-five who are pregnant for the first time have double the rate of miscarriage of women in their twenties, too. (If it is your second or third time around, there is no extra risk.)

These are sometimes the reasons why a baby does not come until a woman is in her late thirties or forties. There may have been a lengthy period of tests and investigations preceding the successful pregnancy. For any woman who is acutely aware that time is running out and who desperately wants a baby, her longing becomes a painful daily reality, and each period like a miscarriage. A couple is under the continual stress of working out ovulation and the right moment for intercourse in spite of their own spontaneous feelings. The burden may become so intolerable that the relationship itself is subjected to strain. Sometimes a period is delayed just long enough for the woman to feel that this time, surely, it must be, but then she experiences the all-too-familiar sensations of the beginning of menstruation.

Susan gave up her job when she was thirty-five, a year after she was married, to improve her chances of conception. Two years later she had a call from her doctor to tell her that her pregnancy test was positive, but she lost the baby within the next few hours. This was followed by a phantom pregnancy in which she had many of the signs of pregnancy, including cessation of periods, abdominal swelling, nausea and vomiting, and what she mistakenly thought were fetal movements. It was a psychological trick in which her body had acted out her passionate desire for a child. As a result, she was very skeptical about any possible pregnancy and, when her fortieth birthday came, decided firmly that she was giving up any idea of pregnancy and went on a twenty-four-mile walk. She conceived the next day. She felt as if in physically walking the notion of having a baby out of her system she had freed her body to become pregnant.

For women who have had frequent miscarriages, or who have experienced many years of infertility and finally—after operations, potentially dangerous drug treatment to produce superovulation, and *in vitro* fertilization—become pregnant in their late thirties or forties, pregnancy is like a miracle. But often it is a miracle that a pregnant woman cannot really trust. At any moment, it seems, the dream could fade and the baby be lost. She may be very dependent upon medical advice and rely on an obstetrician to get the baby safely born, rather than being able to make her own decisions with autonomy and confidence.

She may also have come to think of her body as separate from herself, rather like a car with mechanical problems that has to have parts replaced and the engine tuned by an expert—a specialist in putting the system into running order. It is not surprising that a woman who has gone through investigations and treatment for infertility is often trapped in a relationship with a medical system that is coercive and disempowering.

In traditional cultures, and even in our technocratic society, women who do not reproduce are marked with a stigma. They are often perceived as selfish, odd, or "unnatural." Someone who is pregnant after having tried for a long time to conceive feels she is finally part of the human race, at last like other women. She often has a sense of being drawn into a warm sisterhood with shared concerns. Mixed with anxiety about whether she can get through the pregnancy and give birth to a healthy baby there is joy that the stigma of childlessness is finally erased, and in her transformation from childless woman to "mother."

For many couples, getting pregnant seems to be simpler when they are on vacation and away from their ordinary day-to-day routines. Victoria and Tom were on a Greek island with other couples who had small children: "two adorable little girls at what Tom calls the 'Mary Janes and pinafores stage.' Under the influence of relaxing sunshine and a few bottles of wine, I said, 'Why don't we have another one or two before I'm too old?' " Another couple was on vacation in Portugal, where she lost her pack of contraceptive pills. They decided not to try to get hold of any more. Two others were white-water canoeing, and during the long dark evenings, when there was nothing else to do, made love, came to the conclusion that they would like to have a baby, and made love again!

Reading all this, you may feel that none of these women are like you, and that your motives for having a baby are different and perhaps more complex. Whatever the case, it can be helpful to ask yourself, Why do I want this baby? This is not because you can produce a snap answer or know exactly why you do, but because increased self-awareness, including understanding of those aspects of ourselves that are least salutary, might enable us to be better mothers and more psychologically rounded human beings.

2

Planning Ahead for Pregnancy

Health is not a medical artifact. Economics, politics, the social system in which we live, conditions in the workplace, poisons in the environment, and personal relationships are all elements causing health and disease. Doctors treat illness; they do not make us healthy.

For the vast majority of women, physical health and a sense of well-being during pregnancy have nothing to do with how often they visit the doctor but with the social conditions in which they live—factors like the kind of work they do, their nutrition, and their emotions and relationships.

Women having their first babies over thirty-five have often used contraception for a prolonged period, sometimes since their teens, and they make a conscious decision to stop and get pregnant. They often want to see if they can reduce stress and switch to a healthier lifestyle.

The Pill and Your Diet

Do not plan to come off the pill and get pregnant. Use another method of contraception (a condom for example) for three months, so that there is little chance of hormones from the pill remaining in your bloodstream when you conceive. Oral contraceptives have a systemic effect. Every cell in your body is affected. You need to leave time for it to get back to normal. Artificial progesterone on which the minipill, the most commonly prescribed contraceptive pill, is based can cause masculinization of a female fetus if taken through pregnancy.[1] The incidence of miscarriage and birth defects is also slightly increased.[2]

Oral contraceptives reduce the absorption of vitamins of the B group. When looking ahead to pregnancy, check your diet to make sure that you are getting enough of the foods containing these vitamins. They include liver (no more than once or twice a week), herring, and salmon; brown rice, walnuts, peanuts, wheat germ, and whole-wheat products (such as bread and breakfast cereals); yeast and black molasses. It may be better to avoid liver, however, if you live in a country where animals are still fed estrogens to fatten them up.

Pill users also have a reduced absorption of vitamin C. This in turn may reduce iron absorption and interfere with synthesis of some natural hormones. The best source of vitamin C is fresh fruit, raw vegetables, and baked potatoes in their skins. A large glass of fresh orange juice every day will ensure a good basic level. All green vegetables, including parsley, broccoli, and sweet peppers are rich in vitamin C. Citrus fruits are particularly good sources.

Occasionally folic acid is low in pill users. Alcoholic drinks lower its absorption still further. Low levels of folic acid have been implicated as possibly causing some birth defects, including spina bifida. Include in your daily diet foods rich in folic acid: asparagus, spinach, bran, whole-grain bread and cereals, dried beans of any kind, and yeast. Folic acid is present in liver, too, but again you may wish to avoid it. Low levels of zinc can be raised by drinking a glass of milk every day, since zinc is added to cattle food. Zinc is also present in fresh vegetables, especially peas, and in whole-grain breads and cereals. Use as little cooking water as possible when preparing vegetables or steam them (this conserves the flavor better anyway). Some pill users are also short of another trace element, magnesium. This is found in milk, nuts, and whole-grain products, too.

It is rarely necessary or desirable to take vitamin pills, popular though these are. Excess amounts of vitamins and minerals, especially those that are stored in the body such as A and D, can do more harm than good. Above all, avoid vitamin A supplements after having been on the pill, since excess of this vitamin may be associated with birth defects and vitamin A levels are raised by 30 to 80 percent in women taking the pill. Levels of A take up to three months to return to normal.[3] A nutritious and balanced diet every day is the best protection against vitamin deprivation.

Although some studies have suggested that being on the pill for years reduces fertility, the great majority of women wanting to get pregnant after years on it conceive without difficulty. Perhaps those who do not have always been infertile but did not know it. Occasionally, too, a woman in her early forties does not get pregnant because she is having an early menopause and there are no more follicles inside her ovaries to ripen. If you come off the pill and normal menstruation does not return, check that you are having adequate nutrition in terms of calories. Undernutrition has been shown to reduce fertility. It is a major cause of amenorrhea and failure to ovulate. On the other hand, some women may be slow to rid their bodies of hormones in the pill and be infertile for a year or so after. Some do not menstruate during this time. But even if you menstruate, it does not necessarily mean that you are ovulating regularly.

If after three months off the pill you have started regular periods and notice that your breasts swell at that time, you can take it for granted that you are ovulating. If you are aware of some premenstrual tension, so much the better!

If you have had an intrauterine device (IUD) and it is removed prior to pregnancy, you may possibly be anemic, since anemia from menstrual heavy bleeding is five times more common among women with an IUD than those using other contraceptive methods.[4] If you have a history of heavy bleeding, whether or not you have had an IUD, iron supplements may be in order before you start a pregnancy. Your doctor will be able to tell you this after doing a simple blood test.

Folic Acid

When you or someone closely related has previously had a pregnancy in which the fetus had an abnormality of the central nervous system—spina bifida or anencephaly, folic acid supplementation may prevent the condition if it is taken at the very start of pregnancy. A woman who has had a baby with a central nervous system defect has ten times the chance of having another baby similarly affected. Research in Britain in areas in which there is a high rate of these handicaps, with women who already had babies who suffered from these abnormalities or had pregnancies terminated because the fetus was deformed, suggests that taking extra vitamins and folic acid in capsule form for three months *before* conception and during the first two or three months of pregnancy dramatically reduces the recurrence rate of these conditions. All women who are planning a pregnancy should ensure that they have high levels of folic acid. If in any doubt, it is a good idea to take a .02 to .04mg folic acid supplement every day. Good food sources of folic acid include dark green vegetables, liver, lentils, nuts, cheese, eggs, and milk.

Smoking

Many women who smoke stop well before they become pregnant because they know that smoking increases the risk of miscarriage, premature birth, and a small-for-dates baby (one who is not up to the anticipated size for that particular week of gestation) as a result of a poorly functioning placenta. If a woman smokes, and drinks more than 100g of alcohol and a lot of coffee a week, the baby's birth weight is reduced by 18 percent, compared with the baby of a mother who takes none of these drugs.[5] When a pregnant woman lights up, her baby's heartbeat speeds up, and research shows that for a smoker even to *think* about having a cigarette has an effect on the fetal heart. The baby makes breathing movements in preparation for breathing after birth. When the mother is smoking, oxygen is reduced, these movements cease to be rhythmic, and the baby seems to be literally gasping. There may be long-term effects on the child. Chronic respiratory problems are more common in children whose mothers smoked during pregnancy.[6] A child is much more likely to develop asthma, for example, if the mother, or someone else in the home, smokes.[7] At the age of seven, the children of women who smoked during pregnancy are slightly behind others in reading and some other skills. There is also some evidence to show that babies born to mothers who smoke ten or more cigarettes a day are more likely to suffer sudden infant death syndrome (SIDS)—crib death—than those born to mothers who do not smoke. The risk is increased threefold if the mother is also very anemic. It is thought that this may be because smoking in pregnancy interferes with the normal development of the baby's central nervous system.[8] Smoking increases the rate at which the placenta matures. This may sound like a good thing, but the problem is that in late pregnancy it may mean that the placenta starts to grow old and to deteriorate. The arterial linings of the placenta change and develop a "cobblestone" appearance, and plasma and red blood cells leak out. Parts of the placenta get chalky and do not work any longer. As a result, the baby may be born preterm and be in poor condition.[9] Not only does the placenta mature earlier when a pregnant woman smokes, but the baby's lungs also mature earlier. This means that babies of smoking mothers are at decreased risk of neonatal respiratory distress syndrome (RDS). In spite of this, right through the first year of life the baby is at increased risk of respiratory illness.[10] There is only one advantage in smoking in pregnancy and that is a doubtful one: a smoking mother is less likely to develop preeclampsia. This is a disease peculiar to pregnancy, the symptoms of which are raised blood pressure, albumin (protein) in the urine, and fluid retention. If she does get it, however, she gets it worse than a nonsmoking mother and the outcome for the fetus is worse.[11]

Some fathers now also stop smoking before conception. Chemical poisons in tobacco may produce abnormal sperm, and a pregnant woman should not have to breathe in a smoke-laden atmosphere. This is known as "passive smoking," and there is disagreement about its dangers. But if there is any chance that it could interfere with a baby's health, many mothers should try to avoid inhaling other people's tobacco smoke. Unfortunately it is not considered polite to ask friends and work colleagues to stub out their cigarettes, and it can be embarrassing when you are still in early pregnancy and have not yet told them about it. But some expectant mothers feel forced to do this anyway because the smell of cigarettes makes them feel nauseous. Even if you smoked before, you may be revolted by it in the first three months of pregnancy and can feel trapped in an office or public place, for example, when others light up. Of course you can always lean over your acquaintance's meal and say, "I'm pregnant, and smoking makes me vomit."

Although smoking reduces a baby's birth weight by 3 to 6 ounces, fortunately middle-class women who smoke often have good-sized babies. It is the baby at risk for some other reason, too, who has another condition that interferes with growth *in utero*, for example, or who is indirectly the victim of social conditions in which its mother has to live, who is most likely to suffer from the effects of maternal smoking. Some women are so addicted to smoking that they cannot give it up without causing severe stress. If you have a choice, however, avoid cigarettes for your baby's sake.

Some women who give up smoking in early pregnancy start again when they are waiting for the results of amniocentesis (see chapter 3). Others who smoke lightly find themselves smoking more heavily under the stress of waiting to know whether the baby is all right.

If you are aware of this in advance, you may be less willing to light the first cigarette.

Alcohol

Heavy alcohol consumption is hazardous for the baby. But it has now been discovered that some women cannot safely drink any alcohol at all in pregnancy. Alcohol freely crosses the placenta to the baby; even as few as one or two drinks a week may reduce the baby's birth weight and increase the chances of miscarriage. Much of the research being done on this is retrospective, however, and there may be other factors, such as stress, poor nutrition, and smoking, that contribute to the poor outcome for these babies. Certainly it is known that women who smoke are also likely to drink, and those who smoke heavily are likely to drink heavily, too.

In the United States the fetal alcohol syndrome is a well-known phenomenon in the babies of alcoholic mothers.[12] (It is rare in Britain, as there is less consumption of hard liquor there.) These babies are mentally retarded, growth retarded, and tend to have central nervous system abnormalities and heart problems. They have a characteristic facial appearance with a rather heavy jaw and flattened bridge of the nose.

Although the fetus is vulnerable at any stage of pregnancy, the periods when alcohol most affects brain growth are weeks twelve to eighteen and weeks twenty-four to thirty-six. It is worth thinking through your attitude to alcohol before you become pregnant and deciding what you want to do.[13]

Medicines

Though some drugs are known to have a teratogenic effect (producing congenital malformations) and should never be taken if you are intending to get pregnant, there are a great many others about which little is known. They may be absolutely harmless or, depending on when they are taken and the dosage, one baby in several thousand or fifty thousand or a hundred thousand is affected by them. This is why it is best to avoid all drugs, even over-the-counter household medications like aspirin and indigestion pills, if you are planning on getting pregnant. In practice this is not always possible, and it is then necessary to weigh the benefits and disadvantages of taking a particular drug. Your physician or midwife can help you with this and will have available a list of the drugs that manufacturers recommend not be taken during pregnancy or about which not enough is known to come to any firm conclusions. But if anything is to be prescribed you should tell him or her that you are thinking of starting a pregnancy. It is also wise to throw out anything in the bathroom cabinet that has been prescribed before. If you are away from home and get ill, even if it is just a bout of vacation diarrhea, tell the doctor that you think you may be pregnant and ask whether the prescription is safe for early pregnancy. This is one of the things that ought to be added to foreign-language phrase books!

The first three months of pregnancy are those when the fetus is

Throw out anything in the bathroom cupboard which has been prescribed before

most vulnerable, since it is then that the main structures of the body are being formed. At two and a half months the placenta starts functioning. It is often described as a filter, but in fact it is a sieve that allows through many drugs, depending on their molecular size.

Barbiturates cross the placenta rapidly, can alter the baby's fluid balance, may cause goiter, and, if taken at the end of pregnancy, can interfere with the baby's breathing at birth. They should be avoided in pregnancy. DES (diethylstilbestrol) is the notorious drug that causes a special kind of cancer of the vagina of some daughters of women who have taken it at the beginning of pregnancy. It was used in an attempt to avoid miscarriages but was ineffective at this anyway. Iodides are used for the treatment of thyroid conditions; they cross the placenta and can cause hyperthyroidism (overactivity of the thyroid gland) and goiter (enlargement of the gland) in the baby. Some cough medicines contain large quantities of iodides.

Vaccines

Live viral vaccines may infect the baby. Rubella (German measles) vaccine is of this kind. Check with your doctor to be sure you are immune. If you need immunizing, postpone pregnancy for three months afterward.

Children immunized against polio with oral vaccine excrete the virus and very rarely affect their mothers. If you have never been immunized against polio, you should be immunized at the same time as your child, but first make sure that you are not already pregnant.

Monoamine oxidase inhibitors are psychotropic drugs from which a woman needs to be weaned gradually, best of all before she becomes pregnant, but if not, soon afterward.

If you are diabetic and hoping to have a baby, discuss this with your specialist before you get pregnant. Reserpine, used to lower blood pressure, should not be used in pregnancy as it may slow down the heart rate of the fetus, interfere with the baby's temperature control after birth, and make him drowsy at delivery. Babies of mothers who have been on reserpine may also get swelling of the mucous membrane in their noses so that they cannot breathe. Tetracycline, an antibiotic, is on the list of drugs to be avoided because it can cause a yellow stain on the baby's first teeth and may slow down bone growth. The sulfa drugs, which are used to treat bacterial infections such as cystitis and streptococcal infections, interfere with folic acid synthesis, though they have been used for many years.

Some people think that the more iron you can get, the better.

This is not true, because taking iron pills unnecessarily can produce hemoglobin cells that are so large that they will not pass through the finer blood vessels in the baby. The baby is then deprived of some of the oxygen-carrying blood that would otherwise reach her. The routine administration of iron supplements in pregnancy seems unwise and often causes nausea in the first few months and constipation right through pregnancy. Find out if you are anemic before taking any extra iron.

Aspirin interferes with blood clotting and is suspected of causing birth defects if taken in large doses in the first few weeks of pregnancy. Because it affects blood clotting, if a large amount is taken in the last week before the baby is born, it could cause hemorrhage in the newborn. Low-dose aspirin may be prescribed for some women, however, in an attempt to prevent preeclampsia, the disorder specific to pregnancy that used to be called "toxemia." It appears to be of no benefit for healthy women with normal, or only slightly, raised blood pressure.[14]

Sulfa drugs, used for the treatment of urinary infections, inhibit folic acid metabolism. They should definitely not be taken in the first weeks, and since their safety has not been proved, it is best to avoid them throughout pregnancy. Ergotamine is present in migraine medicines. Since it may cause the uterus to contract, migraine should be treated with alternative drugs and preferably with rest in a darkened room before the symptoms have time to build up.

Sleep medications cross the placenta and are best avoided because they dope the baby along with the mother. Propranolol is used for heart disease but also crosses the placenta and can affect the baby's heart. Sometimes it has to be used, but then only for cardiac disease, not for high blood pressure. Thiazide diuretics used to be very fashionable in pregnancy to reduce water retention, combined with strict dieting to limit weight gain in pregnancy. This is very dangerous.

Several drugs are known to cause damage to the baby's retina when used in high doses. One is chloroquine, used to treat malaria. Another is chlorpromazine, used in the treatment of mental illness, but no damage has been observed with low doses. Diazepam (Valium) crosses the placenta and can cause respiratory depression in the baby, poor muscle tone, and feeding problems. Chlordiazepoxide (Librium) does, too. (These three drugs may have to be used occasionally, nevertheless.) Lithium carbonate crosses the placenta and can alter the fetal fluid balance and cause goiter.

Warfarin is an anticoagulant that crosses the placenta. If an anticoagulant is necessary earlier in pregnancy, it should be replaced by heparin four weeks before the baby is due, since it stops the baby's blood clotting. Heparin, however, does not cross the placenta. Steroids sometimes have to be used in pregnancy for severe asthma, but if alternative therapy works it should be used, as there is evidence of extra risk to the baby. Local and regional anesthetics cross the placenta, too. If you have to have an anesthetic for anything in early pregnancy, let the doctor or dentist know that you think you may be pregnant.

Other Risks

Most people are wary of X rays and realize that they are cancer inducing. If there is any possibility that you might be pregnant or plan to get pregnant before your next period is due, avoid an X ray of the abdomen, pelvis, or lower back. The risk to the baby is highest in the first twelve weeks of pregnancy, and if the fetus is exposed to twenty-five rads or more during this time, termination is advisable. Some people suggest that pelvic X rays, if considered necessary, should be done only in the first half of a woman's menstrual cycle in case she becomes pregnant, but the ovum may be affected whether it is the first or second half. After the twelfth week of pregnancy, it has been estimated that the highest risk to the baby of developing leukemia is in the order of 1 in 500, and it is probably a good deal lower than this.

Toxoplasmosis comes from eating undercooked or raw meat or from handling cat litter. Pass this chore over to someone else before you start a pregnancy, or work out some way of doing it so

RISK OF RUBELLA AFFECTING THE BABY[15]

Stage of Pregnancy from Last Period	Risk of Severe Defect
in first 4 weeks	33%
5–8 weeks	25%
9–12 weeks	9%
13–16 weeks	4%
17–30 weeks	1%

there is no chance of contact. The parasite is also occasionally found in the feces of dogs, rabbits, and pet birds. The woman with primary toxoplasmosis may miscarry or her baby may have birth defects of various kinds, including abnormalities of the brain and hydrocephalus. The chances are, however, that even then the baby will be all right, since eight out of ten babies of mothers with this disease have no symptoms at all.

Check that you are immune to rubella by asking your doctor to do a blood test. The risks of a woman having rubella are well known, and girls are vaccinated against rubella when at school. Women around the age of forty may not have had rubella vaccine, and some will not have had the disease or built up immunity to it. Two or three out of every ten babies born to mothers who have rubella in the first three months of pregnancy either die, have a heart defect, or are blind or deaf. This is a chilling statistic and is why termination is offered to any woman who has the infection at the beginning of pregnancy.

Some studies show that being in a sauna can be dangerous in early pregnancy if your body temperature gets very high and *remains* high.[16] In Scandinavia, people having saunas always get into cold water (or roll in the snow) afterward. For this reason very high temperatures, an extremely hot bath, or lying under a sun lamp for a long time are best avoided. Your own comfort is probably the best guide here. If you run a high fever and think you may be pregnant, it is probably better to take aspirin to get the temperature down, in spite of the disadvantages of aspirin (see page 29), than to allow the fever to continue unabated. If the fever is not high enough to demand anything other than plenty of fluids, a cool room, a tepid bath, and perhaps a bag of ice cubes at the back of your neck or at your temples, perhaps you can avoid aspirin and other fever-reducing drugs. You are the best person to decide.

Your Lifestyle

It is sometimes thought that this kind of information should not be available to women because it makes them unnecessarily anxious. My own view is that I value the facts, that it is my body and my baby, and if I am to understand proposed treatment or investigations, I need information if I am to act as an adult rather than a child.

Moreover, having this kind of information must affect decisions about my lifestyle, things I do every day, which have nothing to do with medical treatment and of which the obstetrician may be unaware. Part of preparing for a baby is to think through the way I live so that I can provide the best start possible for that new human being.

Women often wonder about exercise and whether they should slow down on or give up swimming, hill climbing, long walks, and bicycle rides, or other athletic activities. Research suggests that if you are physically fit you will have developed physiological mechanisms that allow a fetus to tolerate circulatory and respiratory changes occurring with strenuous exercise. The American College of Obstetricians and Gynecologists recommends that a pulse range during exercise of 120 to 140 beats per minute, no matter how fit you are, will improve your fitness without compromising your baby's well-being. The "talk test" is probably the best guide in this.[17] You should be able to continue a conversation while exercising. If you cannot, you are probably overdoing it. The changes that usually occur to cope with exercise during pregnancy are like those during regular athletic training; there is increased cardiac output, stroke volume, heart rate, and blood volume. When you are really exerting yourself, placental blood flow decreases, but the baby takes more oxygen from your blood. Once you have finished

Women often wonder about exercise . . .

long walks . . .

. . . swimming

exercising, more blood flows through the placenta to the baby than before.

Eating for Two

If you think about what an Eskimo mother eats and compare this with a Masai mother's diet, both of whom bear healthy babies, you realize that no strict rules can be laid down about what you should eat and that neither the Eskimo woman's whale blubber nor the Masai blood mixed with milk are essential items of nutrition! Most women benefit, however, from two helpings of a protein food each day. Be generous with fluids, too, since this keeps your bladder and kidneys working well. There is no need to drink milk, although if it is only a matter of disliking it there are many ways of disguising it in other dishes. Eat whole-grain bread and brown rice rather than white. It used to be thought that liver was a near-perfect food for expectant mothers, in order to prevent anemia and give protein. But the liver and kidneys are like filters in an animal's body, and some modern methods of stock rearing and of fattening up animals with hormone-laced feed for quick sale introduce doubts on this score.

A salad as a main course each day is a good rule, with a side salad at another meal. Vegetables make a good main dish with the addition of cheese, eggs, or both; or have a thick vegetable soup followed by whole-wheat or rye bread with cheese. Potatoes are an excellent source of vitamin C if cooked in their skins. A baked potato stuffed with soft cheese with herbs, together with a coleslaw of finely chopped cabbage with apples and nuts, makes a good meal. Have some uncooked fruit every day. Oranges, grapefruit, tangerines, tomatoes, strawberries, and cantaloupe are all rich in vitamin C; and since this vitamin is not stored in the body, it has to be taken in regularly.

Avoid junk foods, including carbonated drinks, packaged mixes, bottled sauces, candy bars, and ready-prepared desserts (just look at the list of ingredients to see why). It is not a bad idea to go through the cupboards in the kitchen and throw out refined foods such as white flour and the containers you collect at the back of the shelf half full of things you never liked anyway. Bear in mind, though, that you probably have a partner who likes his food, too, and a drastic change may be met with resistance. A new cookbook that specializes in recipes for whole foods, but without being self-consciously "improving," may inspire both of you to experiment with dishes.

If your partner has not enjoyed cooking before, now is the time to begin. He needs to be able to produce nutritious and attractive meals quickly, without fuss, and to clear up afterwards. I have sometimes seen it suggested that after a baby is born, women should be content to feed their families on things out of cans, hamburgers and french fries, frozen dinners, and Chinese takeouts. Yet nutrition during breast-feeding is very important if a woman is to feel fit and others in the family are to enjoy their meals. Having a partner who makes good fast food is a health plus.

It is important long before that stage, too, if you have early-morning sickness and evening nausea in the first months of pregnancy. Starvation makes this worse. One way of coping with it is to have frequent nibbles of nutritious foods. So maybe planning for a pregnancy should include a partner's attendance at a course of cooking classes!

Feeling Guilty

A woman may worry right through pregnancy that she has harmed her baby because she did not have the right vitamins or minerals at the beginning, or enjoyed several glasses of wine at a party, or had the occasional aspirin or cigarette, or because she cannot help being under stress because there are money problems, she has a violent partner, or a parent is very ill.

We have seen already that a very poor diet without vegetables and whole grains—a daily diet of hamburgers and Coke that teenagers sometimes have, for instance—especially in the first three months of pregnancy, smoking more than five cigarettes a day throughout pregnancy, heavy indulgence in alcohol, and some drugs used to treat conditions such as epilepsy, can all cause abnormalities in the baby. But older women probably have better nutrition than very young mothers. They find that greasy food gives them indigestion or heartburn when they are pregnant, so they prefer cereals and fresh vegetables and fruit. Many are guided by their own instincts to smoke less, or to give up cigarettes. Sometimes this happens even before they know they are pregnant. If a woman needs medication, doctors who give pregnancy care are aware of the drugs that are dangerous for the developing fetus and usually change them to ones that are safer. So, in realistic terms, most women have no cause for worry. But, of course, we worry anyway.

There is a myth that once upon a time pregnant women simply budded and blossomed, and gave birth to their babies without anxiety. Yet the evidence from women's diaries of the eighteenth and nineteenth centuries reveals that they often worried a great deal—mainly about dying in childbirth, which in those times was a distinct possibility. Women have always feared the impact of unseen, evil forces on the babies growing inside them, too. In many societies the birth of an abnormal baby is seen as punishment for doing wrong. A curse may be placed on a baby by a jealous neighbor. Or the woman may see an omen in nature telling her that her unborn child is afflicted. Women all over the world have used prayers, charms, and ritual to evade evil magic, and have conformed to strict taboos in the hope that they can keep their babies safe. In many ways pregnancy may have been simpler in the past, but for most women it has never been free of anxiety.

3

Will the Baby Be
All Right?

There can be few pregnant women who have not sometimes lain awake in the darkness and wondered whether the baby would be all right. Older women, aware that the risk of congenital abnormalities rises with age, probably worry more than most.

Sometimes people believe that all the screening procedures now available can guarantee a perfect baby. Unfortunately, that is not so. There is still an element of mystery about pregnancy. In fact, this is something that many women value. Although the sperm can fuse with the ovum on a lab table, and the cell cluster that is formed is able to grow in a glass dish, a baby needs a placenta and has to develop in a female body.

You may want the full range of investigations that are available to test whether the baby is in good condition. Or you may feel under pressure to have tests that you do not really want. You have the right to make your own decisions about screening. This is so however old you are and however "high risk" you are rated. Every woman should have the information she needs and be able to come to her own conclusions. These may be different with different pregnancies. One woman said, "With my first child, I was prepared to go ahead with the pregnancy no matter what. This time I felt that I had to take a more responsible attitude toward my own life and well-being. I know how much work babies are this time around, and to have someone who is going to be a baby all their life seems too much to take on." Another said, "I had all the tests with my first pregnancy. The second time I had more confidence in myself. I knew that I could have a healthy baby. I trusted my body. So I decided against screening."

You need not simply put yourself in the doctors' hands. You can make informed choices, valuing doctors as people with information and skills, but not handing over control to them.

Taking Responsibility and Making Decisions

The Western medical culture of childbirth is strongly focused on the assessment and diagnosis of risk, and on the pathology of birth. It is not surprising that women are often anxious and depressed as they go through a variety of tests. It has been estimated, for example, that more than ten thousand women are told it is possible that their babies have Down's syndrome, or Trisomy 21, the most common cause of mental handicap, for each positive case detected.[1] Pregnancy has been turned into an obstacle course. The main weapon against giving birth to a handicapped child is routine and systematic screening of all fetuses, with termination of pregnancy when chances are high that a baby will be handicapped.

When you consider the benefits and hazards of different tests, you need realistic information so that you can weigh the facts and assess risks. You will want to think about the emotional costs of screening and the values that are important to you personally. Counseling should be readily available where screening is done, both before and after the tests. In practice, however, it is often only after a woman has positive test results that she may have the opportunity to talk with a counselor.

You may be certain that you want all available tests so that you can terminate the pregnancy if the baby has an abnormality, and that even tests which involve some risk of miscarriage are worth having when weighed against the possibility of an imperfect baby. Or you may be committed to having your baby whether or not there is a disability, and however severe that disability turns out to be. You may feel that you could never agree to a termination. On the other hand, like many women, you may veer between feeling that you would be silly to refuse the offer of tests, with all that they imply, and feeling protective about your baby and concerned about not getting stuck on a medical conveyor belt of screening and intervention.

Probably most of us are not absolutely sure about these issues. Whatever we decide to do, it almost invariably involves other people close to us, too. Their ideas and feelings about what is right may conflict directly with our own beliefs and emotions. Taking responsibility is not simple. You may find that people are quick to comment in a critical way, and if things go wrong, blame you when your choice is not the one they would have made. There may be times when you feel apologetic, defensive, guilty, or angry.

Medical scientists are eager to penetrate the barriers that separate them from the patient inside the uterus—your baby. Kypros Nicolaides, a specialist in this work, says, "The barrier between the fetus and the obstetrician is being shattered. We now have access to the fetus, and the philosophy of the fetus as patient is emerging." That barrier is, of course, the woman.[2] Tests are now being developed and brilliant medical careers built on research that enables doctors to diagnose conditions in the fetus that were previously undetectable or only suspected. These conditions can rarely be treated at present. A diagnosis may sometimes lead doctors to reduce the length of pregnancy by induction of labor before term, to decide on cesarean section, or in a few large centers to operate on the baby or give a blood transfusion in utero. But screening is not a cure. It usually raises only one question— Should this baby be aborted or not?

As more and more knowledge about the fetal condition is acquired, in the future there will be another question to be answered, too. Like the first, it cannot be answered by doctors alone: What level of handicap is to be considered too severe for a baby to be allowed to survive?

Out of ten thousand boys, thirteen have an extra X chromosome in every cell. This condition is called Klinefelter's syndrome. These boys will grow to be very tall, with arms rather larger than usual, and big hands. Seventy-seven percent of them (compared with 18 percent of all boys) have some learning difficulties, especially in reading, and just under half need speech therapy. Yet two of a group of nineteen Klinefelter boys who were studied into adulthood have university degrees. They are gentle and sensitive, and will be infertile. If genetic tests were not done, most people would never be aware that these boys were in any way different. Would you have a termination?[3]

Many, perhaps most, seriously disabled babies would die shortly after birth if no medical effort were made to save them. In hospitals in the Western world today, these babies regularly survive, often severely mentally and physically handicapped. Dedicated medical and nursing staff are sometimes reluctant to question the urge to treat them with all the sophisticated modern technology at their disposal. In the past, the vast majority would have died within a few days. Now the many who are saved may be subjected to a great deal of surgery. As they grow older, the only place that can cater to their needs may be an institution.

I do not know the answer to the questions I have raised. Perhaps there is no single answer—only the answer that is right for you. But these are the issues that every pregnant woman has to face today.

Down's Syndrome

Ninety-five percent of cases of Down's syndrome are age-related and result from a chromosomal disorder called a "trisomy," which occurs when there is an extra, unpaired chromosome. In every normal cell, forty-six chromosomes are arranged in twenty-three matching pairs. But in Down's syndrome, there is an extra chromosome in the twenty-first pair. Another name for Down's syndrome is Trisomy 21. This is the most common cause of mental handicap. Down's syndrome children have learning difficulties and may also have physical problems. As adults, they often have a happy social life and in a protected environment can take care of themselves, but they remain at the intellectual level of a seven- or eight-year-old.

It is estimated that about half of all babies with Down's syndrome are miscarried early in pregnancy. Although the overall incidence of having a baby with Down's syndrome is 1 in 650 live births, chances are low while you are still in your twenties but start creeping up after thirty-five.

Mother's age	Approximate risk of affected child, 1 per 1,000 live births (1 in . . .)
20	2,000
25	1,205
30	900
35	400
36	290
37	225
38	180
39	140
40	109
41	85
42	70
43	50
44	40
45	32
46	25
47	20
48	15
49	12

If a woman has had a previous Down's syndrome baby, there is a risk of 1 in 100 that another baby will be affected—unless her age-related risk is greater, in which case there is a higher probability. There are other age-related chromosome abnormalities, too, which raise the chances of having an affected baby:

ALL CHROMOSOME ABNORMALITIES[4]

Mother's age	Incidence (1 in . . .)
25	527
30	476
35	204
40	73
45	23

There is a strong case for having screening—a biochemical test, ultrasound, and, if indicated, amniocentesis—if you are forty or older. Most of these tests will turn out "screen positive" purely because of the woman's age. This leads to terrible anxiety, even though there may, in fact, be no extra risk. Before the age of forty the best action is not clear, because the investigation itself introduces a slight risk to the pregnancy. One or two babies in every two hundred are miscarried as a result of amniocentesis. There is a greater risk of miscarriage with twins.

An older woman is more likely to have fibroids in her uterus, and the obstetrician may advise one who is between thirty-five and forty against having amniocentesis in the presence of a fibroid to avoid miscarriage. If you have had previous miscarriages, amniocentesis may be that much trickier.

Ultrasound

Most older women having a baby are likely to be offered ultrasound—and many younger women, too. Ultrasound consists of high-frequency sound waves, too high to be detected by our ears, which are bounced off a solid object—in this case, the baby—and show up as dots tracing the shape of the baby on a screen.

This procedure is usually offered between the fifteenth and twentieth week, although sometimes it is suggested earlier.

Ultrasound tends to be used increasingly to take the place of information that the mother already has and that she is perfectly capable of giving to the doctor. In some hospitals, however, there is a basic distrust of everything a patient says, and reliance is put entirely on machines. Their wholesale use for trivial reasons ("You can have a couple of scans," one obstetrician said. "They are rather fun.") must be questioned if only because they diminish a woman's sense of competence and imply that the mother is a passive object of care.

A scan can confirm pregnancy from about six weeks. Besides ruling out abnormalities such as a tubal pregnancy, it reveals the fetal heart beating and fetal movements. It can also show whether you are having more than one baby, and, if employed in a series, can be used to assess a baby's growth and, shortly before birth, the relation between the baby's head and the mother's pelvis. During the first scan a woman may be asked whether she wants to know the baby's sex, as the person operating the ultrasound may be able to distinguish this. So think in advance as to whether or not you want this information.

The woman is usually asked to attend with a full bladder so that her uterus is pushed upward. She lies down, a glob of gel is squeezed onto her abdomen, and a probe on a metal arm is moved over the uterus. The whole thing takes about ten minutes. Ultrasound is used at this stage to date a pregnancy (plus or minus one week).

It is also used when biochemical tests suggest that a baby may have a neural tube defect (spina bifida or anencephaly—the failure of the baby's brain to grow properly). An anomaly ultrasound scan is usually done at twenty or twenty-one weeks. This is an especially detailed scan to investigate the baby's bones and other organs, tracking the spine for any skeletal abnormality. It can also be used to detect the skin fold at the nape of the neck, to measure the ratio between the distance across the head and the length of leg bones, and reveal a shortened small finger, typical of Down's syndrome. Ultrasound is effective in detecting severe malformation, but there is a risk of false diagnosis. In one trial, 2.4 per 1,000 pregnant women were given a false diagnosis of a malformed baby.[5]

An ultrasound clinic in a hospital tends to be busy, and there may be a long wait before you have a scan, and then again a wait until you can pick up your report. So take something to read. One woman said:

> I was surprised that the clinic was so old-fashioned and functioned in the same way as hospitals used to years ago, with women waiting around for much longer than they should have to, doctors reading out patients' names and then marching off before they'd even made eye contact with the woman. When I had the scan there were two other people in the room, one of whom came in during the scan without introducing herself or saying what her position was. They didn't seem to have read my notes. I had to explain I was there for dating. That was the worst part—that they didn't know why I was there. I was surprised that the hospital, which is supposed to be one of the best, was so archaic in its treatment of women.

Many women like to have their partner or a friend with them. The doctor should explain where the different parts of the baby are as they are located and measured. Some obstetricians have different ideas, however. A family physician who went for her scan had to take her three-year-old with her, because her mother, also a doctor, could not get there in time to look after him, and his father, a doctor, too, was at work. She was told off by the obstetrician doing the scan, who said, "You of all people should have known better."

Seeing the Ultrasound Image

Although ultrasound is obviously a great deal safer than X rays, it must be remembered that X rays were used for many years in obstetrics without anyone questioning their safety, and it was only after they were employed routinely by many obstetricians to measure pelvic capacity that they were found to be carcinogenic. Tests done on ultrasound suggest that there is no hidden danger, but time may teach us differently. We can be fairly positive but not altogether sure.

Some women say that TV programs and articles in magazines give the impression that ultrasound scans are processes in which the woman participates. They look forward to a scan as a way of learning something about the baby. Yet in some hospitals they were expected to lie down, be quiet, and do what they were told. "My questions were either ignored or dismissed," one said. Another woman, "very excited at the prospect of seeing the fetus," said that the radiographer gossiped to her assistant all the way through. "The only consolation I could draw was that she was looking at the screen and there were no sharp intakes of breath! . . . I had the feeling that a tremendous opportunity for letting the mother in on what was happening was missed." She did manage to see the scan, but "for all I know, I could have been looking at a leg of lamb!"

It is often possible to take home a photograph of the image on the screen, but it may look more like a lace curtain with holes in it or a shifting pile of spilled pins than a baby. It can make you wonder what is growing inside you. A woman who took her ultrasound snapshot with her to get her blood test was greeted by a friendly technician who said, "Oh, you've got a photo! Can I see?" The patient watched as she looked at it, frowned, and handed it back with a laugh and the comment, "What *I* say is—you've got a fish in there!" The pregnant woman laughed, too, but I wonder how she felt when she woke up during the night and thought about her baby.

Jan said she felt very scared at having a scan and, when she found she was alone with two technicians she had never seen before, was worried that they would not know what to tell her if something was wrong: "I didn't want to see the fetus, was very tense, and felt my relationship with the baby was private." She is one of many women who wished they had taken their partner or a friend with them.

Although some children eagerly look forward to seeing the scan, others are reluctant—sometimes for the same reasons as their mothers. They are afraid that they will bond with a baby who will never be born because he has a disability. A five-year-old boy said he did not want to see the scan and asked his mother afterwards, "Are you going to have the baby or not?" She was shocked by his question, because she thought it was her problem and did not realize that it was worrying him, too.

You may be disappointed not to see something that looks more like a baby. A woman said she was excited to see her baby's arm waving around. "But it was pretty obvious it had lost its temper. It was certainly an invasion of the baby. The baby didn't like it." Although ultrasound is not invasive of the mother in the sense that it entails sticking a needle into her or poking into her body, the shrill sound it produces that only the fetus hears—and to which it reacts vigorously—certainly suggests that it is invasive for the baby.

Women often like having scans and insist on them. They make the pregnancy more real, and some start bonding with the unborn child on seeing her outlines on the screen. "It was fascinating to see the tiny arms and legs pounding away vigorously even before I could feel any movements," said one woman. "I couldn't have faced an abortion after that; it would have been a terrible decision!" Another woman, whose baby turned out to have serious abnormalities, commented, "It was very upsetting that during the scan I had been shown the heart beating, and here I was two hours later being told the baby would have to go."[6]

Yet seeing your baby on the screen as a balloon-headed, white puppet, with arms and legs like sticks and a spine that seems to be constructed from Legos produces an image that often conflicts with the image a pregnant woman has of the tiny person inside her, the seed unfolding, the soft and gently pulsing creature nestled deep in her body.

You cannot touch and stroke the image on an ultrasound screen. When the fetus reacts to the high-pitched sound with what looks like shock and pain, arms and legs shooting up, the whole body convulsed, you cannot share the baby's distress; you can give no comfort. It may seem as if the baby, and your private awareness of him, has been torn from your body, as if the baby has become a patient to be examined—and you are left empty.

You may resist the idea that you are merely a spectator of the fetus and feel that you want to tuck the image of your baby as a real person inside your body again, and to nurture and love this child in your own way as it develops. Your knowledge about your baby, your complex feelings, all form part of what your baby is. The image on the screen is not objective reality. It is only part of the reality. The other dimensions of reality are bound up with your intimate perceptions of the baby, and with the meaning that this pregnancy holds for you. After an ultrasound you may need to reclaim your baby, and to make this child part of you again.

Alpha-fetoprotein

Alpha-fetoprotein (AFP) is a substance that is synthesized by the baby's liver. It passes into the amniotic fluid and from there into the mother's blood. Levels double every five weeks during the middle trimester of pregnancy. High levels suggest that there may be a central-nervous-system abnormality. Low levels suggest that a woman is at greater risk of having a Down's syndrome baby. There is no level that clearly defines an abnormal pregnancy. AFP concentration varies with the length of pregnancy, going steadily up until it reaches its maximum level at about thirty weeks. Between the sixteenth and eighteenth weeks, the gap between normal and high levels of AFP is greatest, so this is the best time to measure it with a blood test.

You may be advised to have an ultrasound scan to date your pregnancy *before* you have the AFP screening test. Dating is important because a high level might mean that you were later in pregnancy than you thought. It is also high if you are carrying more than one baby and low if you have insulin-dependent diabetes. If the level proves to be especially high or low, you will be recalled after about a week for further tests. This happens to one in twenty women. It is, of course, very worrying, *but most women who have a high or low AFP level have normal babies*. AFP testing is done routinely in some areas, and you may not know you have had it. But it is worth asking about. No test should ever be performed without a woman's informed consent—and without discussion of the implications of a positive result.[7]

Triple Test or Prenatal Risk Profile

A system that has been introduced in some areas to assess the risk of bearing a Down's syndrome baby, one with other chromosome abnormalities, or a baby with spina bifida or anencephaly is a form of biochemical screening called the Triple Test or Prenatal Risk Profile. This is a test of the mother's blood that measures three "markers" in serum: alpha-fetoprotein, unconjugated estriol (uE), and human chorionic gonadotropin (hCG). There is also a Triple Plus Test that uses additional biochemical markers and is more accurate. These biochemical tests are done between thirteen and twenty-three weeks. One woman who was glad she had the Triple Plus Test said:

> They took a large amount of blood. Otherwise it was just like any other blood test. I was pleased that the results would come within a week and they would phone me directly, whether they were good or bad, rather than going through any other health-care worker.

The advantage of these blood tests is that they are only followed by amniocentesis if results indicate that the chances of the baby's having a handicap are higher than usual. So they reduce the risk of unnecessary amniocentesis, which is a highly invasive procedure. But it is important to realize that they are not *diagnostic* tests. They cannot tell you for sure that your baby is handicapped or guarantee that a baby is free of handicaps.

If screening for abnormality is done simply on the basis of the mother's age—testing only women who are over thirty-five, for instance—30 percent of Down's syndrome babies are detected. When this is combined with AFP screening, another 5 percent are detected. But with the Triple Test, 60 percent can be detected, and with the Triple Plus Test more than 80 percent. The Triple Test also detects all babies who are anencephalic (when the baby's brain does not grow) and 80 percent of those with spina bifida.

If you are thinking of having any kind of screening for abnormalities, it is worth finding out exactly what tests are being offered and their level of accuracy.

When a biochemical test reveals that the chances of a baby's having Down's syndrome are 1 in 250 or more, or there is an indication that the baby could have spina bifida, the test is interpreted as "positive." Then it is suggested that the woman have a scan. Every test now in existence gives both false positive and false negative results.[8] False positive results often result in intense anxiety and, occasionally, the abortion of a normal baby. Describing the interval between a positive result from her blood test and having amniocentesis, and then the two-week wait for results after amniocentesis, one woman said, "They told me not to worry. But how could I *not* worry? It was a ghastly time. I cried a lot. I couldn't sleep. I felt drained." Women who have had a false positive screening result may remain anxious even after they have given birth to a normal baby.[9]

By far the most usual reason for a positive screening report is that the pregnancy is not as far along as you thought. Being as little as two weeks off on your dates may change the result. Or you may be having more than one baby. Linda said, "I didn't realize when I decided to have the Triple Test what a lottery it is—there's a chance that they'll diagnose you as probably having a Down's syndrome baby when you're not going to, and then the next step is amniocentesis which has a 1 in 200 chance of miscarriage. So you're on that route into invasive technology."

Cervical Wash or Aspiration

A test is being developed for Down's syndrome that is similar to a cervical smear performed to detect precancerous cells. It can be done as early as the eighth week. Cells from the developing embryo are collected by washing the cervix with a sterile saline solution and drawing the fluid into a syringe. Another, more recent, method is simply to suck out some cells from the cervix with a syringe. These tests are not painful and can be done in a prenatal clinic. The cells are then examined through a powerful microscope to check for abnormal chromosomes.

Amniocentesis

The other common investigation is amniocentesis. This is usually done between the fifteenth and eighteenth week of pregnancy, about fourteen weeks from the probable date of conception. The two extra weeks are added to date you back to the first day of your last menstrual period, which is the only date doctors think you are likely to remember accurately. Some women make up this date for convenience. If you are very unsure it is best to be honest about it, because it can affect the results of the test. Before that time, there is not enough fluid. Putting it off for more than two weeks would entail a more difficult abortion if you should decide on termination, because chromosome culture and analysis usually take another two to three weeks. Amniocentesis can detect chromosomal abnormalities, neural tube defects such as anencephaly and spina bifida, and many errors of metabolism.

You should always be able to speak about any anxieties that you have and get all the information you need with a counselor beforehand. One woman asked the doctor how termination would be done if this were the outcome of the amniocentesis. He dismissed her question with "Oh, let's not be morbid. Let's just do the amniocentesis." She felt put down. This particular doctor is opposed to routine screening on the grounds that it raises women's anxieties unnecessarily. But it appears as if his own anxiety makes it difficult for him to address his patients' anxieties.

An ultrasound scan locates the pool of amniotic fluid, the placenta, and the baby's position. Ultrasound is used to guide the needle into the correct space and to avoid touching the baby. Then a sample of the amniotic fluid in which the baby floats is drawn off through a needle inserted through the abdominal wall and into the uterus. This fluid contains cells that are cast off from the baby and which can be grown to form a culture. Results often do not come for two to three weeks or longer. But geneticists are now starting to use new methods of analysis that produce results in two days.

You feel a prick as the needle passes through the peritoneum covering your uterus and into the uterus itself, and the fluid is drawn off. The whole procedure takes from ten to twenty minutes. Occasionally it has to be done again, but not immediately because the uterus may start to contract. But if you lie quietly for fifteen minutes or so these contractions will fade away. Do not conclude that you have started labor.

Amniocentesis is a method of ruling out about forty different possible abnormalities in the baby, including spina bifida, when part of the spinal column is exposed, and Down's syndrome. There is a 1 percent risk of miscarriage, twice the risk of miscarriage in a pregnancy without amniocentesis. There is a very slight risk of infection. Some babies whose mothers had amniocentesis have breathing difficulties at birth and others have orthopedic problems (club foot, in particular). Occasionally a false positive diagnosis results in the termination of a pregnancy with a normal baby; but this is rare.

It is important to realize before amniocentesis that it is not a question of sticking in a needle like a coin in a slot and coming up with an answer. You will probably feel anxious, and it is a good idea to go with a friend—especially if you know someone who has been through it before. Liz, for example, went with a friend who was two months ahead of her, "and we were able to boost each other afterwards." All went well, but she says she began to worry when the woman before her came out saying that they could not get enough fluid after trying four times, and she had to return in two weeks. This was unusual—most units will try twice and, if unsuccessful, will reschedule the procedure for another day.

> "I disliked intensely the sensation of the needle going in to retrieve some fluid. The doctor made two attempts to get fluid and still couldn't get any," Angela said. "I would have had to go back two weeks later. I decided against it. The incident made me feel tremendously protective toward my child. The needle in my stomach felt so threatening."

Another woman expressed her distaste of amniocentesis as an intrusion on the intimacy of her pregnancy: "I felt the baby's privacy had been invaded with this needle going into its amniotic sac."

Helen says that amniocentesis was "an appalling experience," made worse because she dreaded it and knows she "tensed up." It wasn't helped by the lecture from the doctor on the risks of amniocentesis and being asked to sign the consent form, although this should always be done. But many women find it all far simpler than they expected. Emma said that her consultant introduced the needle very low down, after shaving off a small patch of pubic hair:

> I felt a couple of tiny pinpricks and thought they were just the preliminaries. The consultant commented to the midwife that the

abdomen was rather tough and he was having difficulty getting the needle through. I still thought this was for the local anaesthetic. Then I felt a niggling sensation deep inside. It suddenly dawned on me that this was the actual amniocentesis procedure itself.

You may find that the needle leaves a painful bruise, especially if more than one insertion has to be made. It will disappear after a few days and does not mean that any harm has come to the baby, although you may experience some discomfort if you have an older child who likes to climb all over you. After amniocentesis, take it easy if you can for the next twelve hours. Sometimes afterwards at home a woman notices bleeding or leaking of amniotic fluid. If this happens to you, call whoever performed the test to let them know. Bleeding and fluid discharge usually abate without causing problems, but you will probably feel happier if you can rest in bed.

The baby's heart will be checked before you have the amniocentesis, and again afterwards, and it is comforting if you have a chance to see the baby moving on the ultrasound scan after the amniocentesis has been performed. You can ask for this if it is not suggested.

If you are rhesus (Rh) negative, there is a chance of some of the baby's blood crossing the placenta, so you are given an injection to prevent the buildup of antibodies in your blood which may adversely affect the baby.

Chorionic Villus Sampling (CVS)

An alternative to amniocentesis, and one that can usually be performed earlier in pregnancy, is CVS. This diagnoses the same disabilities. Guided by ultrasound, a sample of tissue that forms the sac surrounding the embryo is extracted, either through the vagina or under local anesthesia, through a small nick made in the woman's abdomen. There is less risk of introducing infection with the abdominal route. There is a 2 percent risk of miscarriage as a result of the test. But there is a 2 to 3 percent risk anyway at the stage of pregnancy when this is done—between ten and twelve weeks.

Ninety percent of women go on to have successful pregnancies after amniocentesis, 86 percent after CVS. One problem is that an apparent abnormality may be revealed that affects the placenta, but not the fetus. This may be minor. An unnecessary termination may then take place.

One women who chose CVS said, "It was uncomfortable, but not as much as having an IUD fitted. I lost a bit of blood afterwards—like a light period." Her pregnancy was straightforward and the baby normal.

The advantage of CVS compared with amniocentesis is that it can be performed earlier than amniocentesis is usually done, thus enabling the woman to have a much earlier and therefore simpler abortion if an abnormality is detected.

Complications of CVS include infection, bleeding, and, possibly, damage to the placenta or the baby's limbs. The Medical Research Council European collaborative trial to assess the safety of this technique revealed that women who had CVS were 4.6 percent less likely to have a live baby than those who had amniocentesis, usually because they gave birth to a very preterm baby.[10] We do not know if there may be long-term effects of CVS, because the research has not yet been done.

Calculating the Risks

Although an older mother is at increased risk of having a baby with a chromosome abnormality such as Down's syndrome, there is no specific reason why she should be more likely to bear a child with malformation of the central nervous system such as spina bifida.

Women having late pregnancies are often frightened of the possibility of a mentally handicapped baby, particularly one with a severe condition who survives for many years. "I don't know how we'd cope. It's the worst and most worrying question of all. Will our life become lifeless for ten, twenty years? Will we not exist because the child doesn't really mentally exist?" Sometimes they dread this so much that they cannot talk about it, as if, somehow, the words could create the fact.

They may dream of having a baby that is not "right," although the mental pictures with which they disguise the image of the baby mean that they may not recognize the dream as anything related to the pregnancy. Dreams about having done sloppy work or produced an object that is imperfect and criticized by others (often people in authority or in uniform) seem to be one way in which a woman wraps up her fears of having an abnormal baby. These dreams, when remembered, produce a wave of distress that seems out of all proportion to the incidents that occurred. Sometimes the dream is about baby animals that are disposed of or drowned because other people decide they are unwanted or not good enough. Dreams of losing a part of your own body that has something wrong with it can also be dreams about the baby. It may be a tooth or limb. In pregnancy, especially after you feel movements, the baby is like a part of yourself.

Knowing that disturbing and often vivid dreams are a normal part of pregnancy can be reassuring, if only because you then feel less odd. Women often do not talk about these things because they are afraid they will be upset, and even introduce ideas into other pregnant women's minds and start them worrying. In fact, a substratum of anxiety, a sense of "What if . . . ?" "How could I cope if . . . ?" is common in pregnancy and can be useful mental preparation for the psychological challenges that come with being a mother. None of your anxiety is being wasted; it is all grist for the mill.

Women who feel fit during pregnancy may be less nagged by doubt about the baby being normal because they know their bodies are working well. Some are vibrant with health and well-being. Many older mothers are surprised by this and describe with delight long walks, swimming into late pregnancy, enjoying sex (sometimes in a new way), and having softer skin and shinier hair than usual.

It is very different for a woman who spends much of the first three months of pregnancy with nausea and vomiting, or feeling exhausted. She asks herself whether this must not be harming the baby and is a sign that something is wrong. Her anxiety is increased, until it may become part of a spiral that is not only the result of her digestive disturbance and tiredness but also tends to increase it. When a rundown state persists after twelve weeks or so and is not cured by extra rest and sleep, it often continues until about the sixteenth week, the time when amniocentesis is performed, and disappears thereafter. Once a woman knows that her baby is unlikely to have a congenital abnormality she can relax and enjoy her pregnancy.

It is also different for a woman who has lost a previous baby. One whose last baby had lived only for a week and who is seven months' pregnant, says:

> I have either had, or imagined I had, every possible complication there is. My husband and I have only just started discussing possible names and where on earth there is going to be room for a crib in our bulging house. A friend said to me, "So you've finally accepted that you're pregnant," and I realized that no one apart from the children had really been allowed to talk about it.

Keeping the Secret

The psychological costs of screening are often underestimated. Many women do not feel they can tell other people—colleagues at work and members of the family—about the coming baby until after they have had the screening results. It is as if they are not having a baby at all, in spite of the physical changes. Sometimes a woman refuses to acknowledge a baby's obvious kicking until test results have arrived because she is afraid that she will bond with an imperfect baby, whom she then must abort. To have to cope with morning sickness, or evening sickness (which is almost as common), to be unable to go more than a couple of hours without a cookie or a banana, to feel unutterably weary and drag through each day longing for bed, and then not to be able to sleep without interruption at night because of pressure on your bladder—all while the pregnancy is hidden from family and colleagues at work—can be an intolerable burden.

If conception was accidental, an older expectant mother may feel that something must be wrong with the baby. It is as if *thinking* about starting a baby makes it safer. This holds true if it means giving up smoking and having sensible nutrition before conceiving. But a happy accident need not put a baby at risk. Phyllis felt that her baby's conception had been "freakish." She had been working hard, switching between two demanding jobs, and her husband had just gotten over the flu. Amniocentesis set her fears to rest. A woman who already has a family may fear that this time it is not going to work out as it should: "When you have two or three healthy children, you wonder if you are pushing your luck by having another one."

When pregnant women in one area of England were asked whether they would have an abortion if it was discovered that a baby had a serious abnormality, 70 percent said that they would continue the pregnancy.[11] In fact, if an abnormality is detected, the majority do decide on termination. So when faced with reality, 30 percent of women make a decision that conflicts with their own values. This conflict, which is concealed within the concept of fetal screening, may cause anxiety, anticipatory grieving, depression, and guilt. The tests a woman is offered are often seen as "just for reassurance," but when it comes down to it, they are the first steps on a course of action that may finish with a diagnosis of abnormality and often the abortion of a much-wanted baby.

When at last it is known that the chances of the baby's being mentally handicapped are slight and the pregnancy can be given social recognition, the whole thing becomes easier. Many women say they felt a load off their minds. One woman said, "I felt as if a great weight had been lifted, and I realized just how worried I had been." No tests can assure you that the baby is perfect, however, although they can rule out specific abnormalities.

You may feel that there is no point in having amniocentesis if you would not want your pregnancy terminated anyway. On the other hand, you may believe that it is better to be prepared, and that knowing that the baby has a disability would help you cope better after the birth. A woman who was told that her baby had a rare form of dwarfism and would probably not survive birth decided to go ahead with the pregnancy: "It was like living with a terminal illness. It gave me the time I needed to prepare myself for Adam's death."[12] It is important to think through how you feel about termination. Some women say that their doctors assumed that they would automatically have an abortion if there were an abnormality. "It was taken for granted that a termination was necessary," one woman said. "I am angry that we were given no choice about it. The decision ought to have been ours alone." Whatever decision you make, it is *yours*, not the doctor's.

Waiting for Results

After amniocentesis, there follows the stressful period of waiting two weeks or more to get the diagnosis. Anna said this was "horrible" and she felt in limbo. A woman who had to wait a full month commented that it was "like waiting for exam results." In about 1 percent of cases a culture cannot be grown and the test either has to be done again after another couple of weeks or, if the woman is more than twenty weeks pregnant, it may be decided to obtain a fetal blood sample, which will give a far less accurate result in two or three days, or to skip it completely—in which case she still does not know one way or the other.

Fetal cells obtained from amniocentesis will also tell whether you are having a boy or a girl. This is only important medically if there is the possibility of a sex-linked inherited disease such as hemophilia or Duchenne's muscular dystrophy. It is usually up to you whether or not you wish to be told the sex of your baby. Some women want to keep it a surprise and believe that knowing in advance makes the pregnancy less "normal." Occasionally an obstetrician has a policy of never telling a woman because he does not trust her not to try and terminate the pregnancy if the baby is the "wrong" sex. With technological power come new responsibilities, ones that should be exercised by parents and not only by professionals.

Fetal Blood Sampling

Another method of testing for genetic defects is fetal blood sampling, or cordocentesis. A needle, directed by ultrasound, is inserted into the baby's umbilical cord and blood drawn off so that it can be analyzed. It used to be done through the vagina, but there is a risk of infection this way; so when it is done now it is usually through the abdominal wall.

This technique was introduced in the 1980s to test for hemophilia and other blood and metabolic disorders, immunodeficiencies (conditions in which a baby cannot resist infection), and toxoplasmosis—the disease caught from contact with cat litter or infected raw meat. Although harmless in adults, toxoplasmosis can damage the unborn baby's nervous system.

This invasive technique has become less popular with doctors and pregnant women now that most of these disorders can be diagnosed in early pregnancy by chorionic villus sampling or, a little later, by amniocentesis.

With fetal blood sampling there is a 1 to 3 percent rate of miscarriage. But when a woman has a "high-risk" pregnancy—and many older women are placed in this category—the rate of miscarriage is significantly higher.

A Termination

On the front page of each newsletter of the British organization Support After Termination for Abnormality there are these words: "The decision to terminate a wanted baby because of fetal abnormality is one made out of care for the unborn child and in consideration of existing family. It is not a decision taken easily or lightly."[13]

It may be the most difficult decision a woman ever has to make, and the pain of making that choice, and of being the person who has to make it, may bring intense suffering. It can be difficult to get any information about how termination is done and what the experience is like. One woman said, "Nobody is willing to talk about termination till you get to the final stages of believing that there's something wrong. That's why women need midwives, not just doctors who discard our worries." A late termination means an induced labor. Be warned that it may take twelve hours or longer. You will need a strong and loving companion with you. You may decide that it would be a good idea to make a birth plan. A woman having a termination is given a single room, but it may be on a labor ward, where other women are giving birth to healthy babies, or on a gynecology ward, where women are having social terminations and sterilizations.

When a woman has already felt her baby moving, the knowledge that it has Down's syndrome or a central nervous system anomaly, and the decision to terminate the pregnancy, are especially distressing. Some women say that everything they do comes automatically and when the news is given to them it is like pressing a button to start an inevitable process for which they were mentally prepared all along. It is not so much a question of "Why is this baby abnormal?" but "How could I have ever thought that I could bear a normal baby?"

If you are told that your baby has an abnormality, your first reaction is likely to be one of shock and bewilderment. You may not be able to understand or believe what you are hearing. It seems as if it must be happening to someone else, that you must have been given another woman's results, or that the hospital has made some other awful mistake. You may feel paralyzed.

Some women say that they reacted by feeling that if only they could go home everything would be normal again; some cannot stop crying; others freeze emotionally and are not able to cry. The question a woman asks herself over and over again is "Why *me*? Why *my* baby?" She usually blames herself for what has happened and feels that if she had done something different, or avoided doing something, her baby would be normal. She may feel like a failure as a woman. It may be as if she is the only person to whom this has happened, and she is trapped in utter isolation and loneliness. But there is also anger, and sometimes a desperate need to blame someone else.

It may be terribly difficult to face other people, and even to go out of the house—to talk about what you are going through with family and friends, to explain to the childbirth teacher, your mother, and perhaps your other child.

Men often feel that they must not cry and have to be strong. It can seem for a woman as if her male partner is refusing to share the grief and is just concentrating on his own life and his own interests. Trying to deny reality, working furiously, refusing to think or to talk about the painful experience are ways of grieving.

Most women have not revealed the pregnancy to people at work and many have not told close family members either, so they feel bound to put a brave face on it and carry on as usual. They feel very alone. They often say they needed an understanding person to talk with after receiving the news and before having a termination—and then again in the weeks that follow. Many hospitals provide counselors. If you can, contact a group of patients who have gone through the experience themselves. There may be someone who can give one-on-one emotional support.

After a Termination

Women often say that it helped to be able to see the baby and, if they wished to, to have some quiet time to hold it and to say good-bye. The hospital will then help to arrange a funeral if that is what you want. You should give yourself time to grieve. The need to grieve is often unacknowledged, but it is as necessary as breathing.

One woman said:

It is thanks to the midwife's care and handling of us and her gentle persuasion that we were prepared to see our baby, even though at the outset this was a proposition we could not even contemplate. The midwife came back in and gently asked us if we wanted to see him. She said that if she described him it might not seem so frightening. She described him beautifully and said that she enjoyed holding him. We both knew that we had to see him, thanks to her. It would, after all, be the last time that we three would ever be together.[14]

Suzanne was told by a doctor that at thirty-seven she did not come within the age group for which amniocentesis was available. "I was strong and experienced," she says, "and asked if I might have an appointment with the chief of obstetrics, who readily agreed to make the arrangements." She went back three weeks later for the results: "I had deliberately resisted any involvement with the fetus—difficult—but I knew I would terminate if anything was grossly wrong." The baby had Down's syndrome. "Though I had long imagined facing this news and slipped into the pattern I had prepared for myself, I was emotionally affected more than I expected. We coped with paperwork, and I asked for a quick admission." She only had to wait twenty-four hours but wonders how she would have managed without a supportive husband and doctor. The termination was efficiently and sympathetically done. She feels that someone should have told her that at this stage of pregnancy her body would react as if she had borne a live child and that she would lactate.

After a termination for abnormality, a woman may find that she is left alone to cope. In Britain, for example, there is no statutory aftercare following a birth before twenty-eight weeks. Home visits and concern and practical help from a midwife and doctor would be signs that the woman's experience of pregnancy, birth, and loss was acknowledged. As it is, the grieving woman is often left to move on as well as she can, while at the same time she is bleeding, her engorged breasts are like soccer balls, and her whole body has to adapt to the same rapid change as after a birth.

In the past, a woman who delivered a dead baby would have had estrogen pills to suppress her milk. This is no longer done because of the risk of postpartum hemorrhage (bleeding after delivery) and thromboembolism (a blood clot that breaks off and blocks a blood vessel). It was never particularly effective, anyway, and when the estrogen was stopped the women often became engorged again. A better way is to bind the breasts tightly or wear a good bra, use cold compresses (ice cubes in a face towel or large handkerchief are comforting), and take analgesics if your breasts are painful. Vitamin B6 in 200mg doses has been shown to reduce engorgement for nine out of ten women. It is effective in about eleven hours and should be taken for five days.

Expressing milk encourages the supply, but on the third and fourth days, when your breasts are likely to be most hot and swollen, kneeling in a hot bath with breasts suspended in the water allows the milk to stream out without providing extra stimulation.

To have milk pouring from your breasts when you have no baby to feed is as if your whole body were weeping. For some women there is a peculiar comfort in being able to surrender their bodies completely to grief in this way. Suzanne decided not to attempt another pregnancy:

Physically I feel able to cope with termination again but it was such a difficult emotional experience I'm not certain I would want it. I had expected to value life a lot less after depriving something of life, but exactly the opposite reaction occurred.

Other women have gone on, after a breathing spell and a time of grieving for the lost baby, to embark on another pregnancy, have had screening again, and have given birth to normal, healthy babies with enormous gratitude and delight. They sometimes say that they did not really let the grieving go until they had had another baby: "I didn't get the longing out of my system until Deirdre was born."

Sometimes a loving partner, anxious to protect a woman from the suffering involved, does not agree to another pregnancy. She may see this as a lack of confidence in her. It is as if he is accusing her of not being able to cope. She may resent him for treating her like a child and feel rejected. The two move into their separate emotional worlds.

This was what happened to Sally and Tom. She accused him of being "insensitive" and "cruel." She wrote:

> He was adamant that another disaster could not be allowed to occur and within three months had a vasectomy. He was totally unable to comprehend my wish for another baby which might lead to an abortion and more sorrow. We sought advice on artificial insemination but he backed out. So we are now left, often at loggerheads, and at best pushing away the fact that I still resent him.

This kind of pain can be experienced even when there are other living children. The Down's syndrome baby was Sally's twelfth child.

After she had lost the baby, one woman realized she had shut herself away from her partner's pain because it was more than she could handle and witnessing his suffering sharpened her own ordeal. She exerted a tremendous effort of will to be cheerful because she wanted to show him and her parents that she had "come to terms" with the experience. Tears welled up after she had locked the bathroom door, but she never allowed herself to cry in front of him. Looking back on it, she feels she made things more difficult for both of them. "After about a week I realized he was suffering with no support from me. I'd actually forgotten I wasn't suffering alone." Then they began to cling to each other and to share the grieving. This itself brought healing.

Following a termination for fetal abnormality a woman may feel very vulnerable and fearful. Kate said she was afraid of everything—"Of getting pregnant again, of going on long-distance trips, of flying in planes. I've become very afraid of death. I'm afraid I'll be punished for taking a life and that somehow I'll have to pay for it."

It took some time for her fully to accept her thoughtfully made decision to abort her Down's syndrome baby. As her fear ebbed she was left feeling differently about many things, especially how fragile human life is. For many months she could not face sex because of her panic at the idea of going through it all again. Then she and her partner began to reach out to each other and found comfort in sex. Now she is looking forward with excitement to another baby.

4

Prenatal Care

There are wide cultural variations in prenatal care. In the United Kingdom everyone has full health coverage under the National Health Service. They pay only for prescribed medications, and many people—the elderly, children, those receiving state benefits, and pregnant women—are exempt from these payments. Maternity care is free of charge. It takes different forms, depending on whether a woman is estimated to be at high or low risk, and on her own choices. A pregnant woman may attend a prenatal clinic with a "community midwife" attached to the clinic of her GP (a general practice physician). She may go to a clinic at a hospital, where she sees midwives and obstetricians, and this is most likely to happen when she is considered "high risk." Or she may have "shared care" divided between the GP clinic and the hospital. Or, alternatively, she may have care almost entirely from a small team of midwives, unless they refer her for specialist advice. Midwives are the main caregivers for all but a small minority of women who choose to book with a private consultant obstetrician, and to pay for maternity care.

The status of midwives varies widely, too. In Italy and Spain, for instance, where there are far too many obstetricians, most must act as attendants to obstetricians, follow their instructions, and call them when delivery is imminent. Only in outlying rural areas is it usual for midwives to assist at births themselves. In Scandinavian countries midwives have much greater responsibility. Swedish midwives, for example, have full professional status. If delivery is difficult, a midwife may do a vacuum extraction (suck the baby out with an instrument like a small vacuum cleaner). In Eastern Europe midwives tend to have low status, and the systems in which they work are very hierarchical. But in the Netherlands, midwives have their own practices and care for the majority of women with normal pregnancies. Thirty-eight percent of women there give birth at home. Midwives work in a variety of settings and are legally bound to assist a woman at birth whoever she is, and wherever she is. Most British women give birth in the hospital, but this may be a small GP unit outside a general hospital—like an American birth center, or in a GP unit within a larger hospital. Less than 2 percent give birth at home. There are variations on this theme, and often new ventures in maternity care given by midwives in other European countries, as well as Australia and New Zealand.

In the United States, where there is no universal health-care coverage, most women pay for health insurance. Most of them receive prenatal care in clinics or private offices from a group of obstetricians, or to a lesser degree, a group of midwives or family physicians. The poor, who receive government financial assistance with health care, or who have no health-care coverage, attend clinics located within hospitals or community clinics affiliated with a hospital. There they are seen by a nurse and the doctor or midwife who happens to be on call that day. Most middle-class American women give birth in a hospital, cared for by a doctor or midwife from their group. Some choose to give birth outside the hospital in birth centers or at home, attended by midwives. The poor usually give birth in the hospital, attended by student doctors or midwives who are supervised by fully trained physicians or midwives.

In Canada, there are few midwives, and most women (all of whom are covered by government health insurance) are cared for prenatally and during birth by their family physician or obstetri-

Take a good book or team up with a friend

cian. There are no government-approved out-of-hospital settings
for birth, although a few women choose to give birth at home with
midwives, most of whom are practicing outside the law. Canada is
changing, however, and some provinces have already or are about
to legalize midwifery and home birth.

Understanding what goes on during prenatal care is important
if you are to have accurate information on which to base decisions.
At your first appointment, tests and history taking will be more
time-consuming than later appointments. You will be interviewed
by a doctor or by his nurse (or in some hospitals by a staff doctor),
and it would be a good idea to contact him or her if any worries
develop or if you have unanswered questions. The doctor or nurse
will ask the first day of your last menstrual period (LMP) and
whether you have a regular menstrual cycle and its length. This is
so that the expected date of delivery (EDD) can be worked out, by
adding seven days and nine months to that day. Avoid guessing a
date for the start of your period earlier than it may have been, as
induction of labor may be proposed because you appear to be
overdue.

Your caregiver will want to know about operations and illnesses
you have had, including urinary infections (such as cystitis), rubella, sexually transmitted diseases (including nonspecific ure-
thritis and thrush), and any medications you are taking. The
obstetric history includes all previous births and abortions,

whether they were spontaneous (miscarriages) or induced. Let her know if you had any pregnancy problems or birth complications before. You may also be asked questions about the health of your own family and whether any of them suffers from high blood pressure or diabetes, and she may ask whether there are twins or triplets in the family. She will probably ask if you smoke, and if so, how many a day and how many alcoholic drinks you usually have. If you are not married, there may be detailed questions about housing and your plans for the future, and you can also ask to have a talk with the social worker.

Someone will weigh you, as they will at subsequent visits, too, and measure your height. The range of possible weight gain in pregnancy is wide, and there is no single "right" or "normal" gain. The largest weekly gains usually occur in mid-pregnancy. If you gain a good deal then, it does not mean that you will continue to put on as much until the end of pregnancy. This is not the time to diet by cutting down on nutrition, though if you are gaining weight too rapidly for comfort, it is a good idea to omit sugar, including "invisible" sugar in sauces, canned foods, drinks, and other dishes in which there is invisible sugar. Although if you gain little weight you are more likely to have a lower-weight baby than if you put on a lot, women who gain none at all have babies who are only 9 to 12 ounces less than those who gain a great deal.

The urine specimen is another regular part of the prenatal visit. It is tested for the presence of glucose (which occurs in diabetes and prediabetic conditions), protein (one of the signs of preeclampsia), and bacteria (produced by a urinary infection). You may be asked to produce a midstream sample of urine, which is done by interrupting the stream of urine with a strong pelvic-floor contraction and then letting the second flow of urine go into the container provided.

Your blood pressure will also be taken, using a sphygmomanometer. In early pregnancy blood pressure is down to lower than normal: the upper figure, the systolic, a little bit, but the lower, the diastolic, well below the nonpregnant level. During the seventh or eighth month, the diastolic pressure rises to your more usual level, and under stress, the upper figure, which is readily affected by strong emotion, may be high (if you are anxious or angry or have had to rush to your appointment, for example). It may be taken for granted that you want an ultrasound scan, or a series of scans. Some obstetricians use scans routinely and tell women that they are completely harmless, although we cannot possibly know whether this is so until research into possible long-term effects has been done and accurate records kept of exposure. Unfortunately, neither of these things is happening.

Preeclampsia

Preeclampsia is a disease that only occurs in pregnancy. Signs and symptoms include puffiness (edema) of ankles, hands, and face, severe headache, abdominal pain, vomiting, and visual disturbances, and on examination, raised blood pressure and protein in the urine. In mild preeclampsia, which occurs in about 10 percent of all pregnancies during the last few weeks, without harming the baby, blood pressure rises to about 140/90. Some doctors pay more attention to how much your blood pressure has increased over your lowest reading than to how high it gets. If your systolic rises thirty beats or more and your diastolic fifteen beats or more, they consider it preeclampsia. The lower figure is the more important one, as it is the resting pressure between heartbeats. In about 2 percent of pregnancies, preeclampsia is severe and the upper figure approaches 160, the lower 100, even when you are resting in a bed. First-time mothers are more likely to develop preeclampsia than those having second or subsequent babies. Even if you have only had a miscarriage before, you are probably protected from preeclampsia, though not if you are pregnant by a new partner.

In preeclampsia, the blood flow from the mother to the placenta is reduced. Researchers are now convinced that although the rise in blood pressure—which is often the first signal that anything is wrong—comes in late pregnancy, preeclampsia is caused very early in pregnancy by damage in the tissues that later form the placenta. The hypertension (raised blood pressure) results from an imbalance between hormones that make blood vessels tighten and other hormones that make them relax. Clinical trials of supplementation with calcium, magnesium, and fish oil are taking place. More than nine thousand pregnant women in seventeen countries have collaborated over five years with a project to discover whether a "baby" aspirin a day helps to prevent preeclampsia. The idea is that aspirin makes blood less sticky and prevents it from clotting so easily; then it can flow better. But taking it in pregnancy could mean that the placenta is more likely to separate from the lining of the uterus, with the result that bleeding occurs during pregnancy, the woman bleeds too much at the time of birth, or—because the drug crosses the placenta—the baby is harmed in some way. Unfortunately, results of this trial reveal that aspirin does not save babies' lives.

At the first appointment, your heart is usually checked with a stethoscope, and at the same time breasts and nipples are examined. If your nipples are inverted, there is a good chance that their shape will change during pregnancy, and even if there is little alteration, once you get the baby firmly fixed onto your breast he or she will draw the nipple into the back of the mouth and mold it into the right shape. If you want to help the whole process, suggest to your partner that love play should include plenty of manual and oral stimulation of your nipples. You do not need to do anything else.

At the first visit some blood is taken so that your hemoglobin level can be checked. If it is below ten at the twelfth week of pregnancy, you are anemic. Your blood group is recorded in case you need a transfusion and so that any problems associated with being Rh-negative or ABO can be anticipated. The blood is also tested for sexually transmitted disease and antibodies to rubella. You are given an internal examination to feel the size of your uterus and cervix, and you may be offered a cervical Pap smear to detect any precancerous cells. A better time may be *after* you have the baby.

When you are lying on the table being examined by the doctor or midwife, he or she may look at your legs to see if you have varicose veins and, later in pregnancy, for any swelling (edema, a sign of fluid retention). The abdomen is palpated to see where the top of the uterus lies. The height of the fundus (the top of the uterus) in relation to the pubic bone at the front of the pelvis is one way of estimating the length of gestation.

The Baby's Movements

Most women who are Rh-negative are offered an injection of RhoGAM (anti D immune globulin) at twenty-eight weeks, to prevent their blood from developing antibodies to their baby's Rh-positive blood cells. The reason caregivers worry about these antibodies is that once they have developed, they cross the placenta and destroy some of the baby's red blood cells. Before RhoGAM, many Rh-positive babies died because of the blood incompatibility with their Rh-negative mothers. RhoGAM may also be offered to Rh-negative women after miscarriage or abortion, after amniocentesis or chorionic villus sampling, and within a couple of days after birth. Each of these events represents situations in which the mother is likely to develop antibodies to Rh-positive red blood cells. The antibodies remain in her blood and are present in future pregnancies.

At each visit, the baby's heart rate will be checked. This can be done using a small Doppler ultrasound apparatus about the size of a cassette recorder, called a sonic aid or simply a "Doppler." With the sound turned on, you can hear the baby's heartbeats yourself. After thirty weeks or so, other tests of the fetal heart rate may be suggested, especially if there are any questions about the baby's development or well-being. Prenatal cardiotocography (ACT) or electronic fetal heart rate monitoring (EFM) may be used to check the baby's heart rate response to its own movements, called the Non-Stress Test (NST); to a loud sound made next to the uterus, called the Fetal Acoustic Stimulation Test (FAS); or to uterine contractions induced by intravenous oxytocin or by breast stimulation, called the Contraction Stress Test (CST). It is considered reassuring if the baby's heart speeds up with movement and with loud noise, and if it remains the same during contractions. The results of these tests are not completely reliable, however. Before consenting to the test, be sure to find out why it is being suggested and what clinical decisions will be made on the basis of the results.

Through your awareness of your baby's movements, you get to know about and be in touch with him in a very direct way. In the recent past, with the emphasis on modern obstetric technology, the mother's knowledge of her unborn baby's activity, his cycles of sleep and waking, and the location and nature of his movements, has been largely ignored and considered irrelevant beside the "scientific" evidence concerning placental function from blood tests, electronic fetal monitors, and the ultrasound scans and other ways of getting windows into the womb, which are now employed in almost every obstetric unit. The mother has a unique opportunity, however, to get to know her baby and to be aware of him throughout the twenty-four hours in a way that is impossible for any outsider. Abigail Lewis, writing of her own pregnancy, says of the fetus:

> It stretches and turns; its movements gain in power and direction. Whatever may be your own doubts about where mankind is heading and what maturity is, the fetus seems to feel no doubt at all as to what it wants; and in all that curious, segregated, seemingly static chunk of a year, you become aware of a new kind of time, the fetus's time, the slow pushing time of growth.[1]

The fetus is a water-baby in a fluid-filled capsule. Though the mother does not usually feel movements until about four and a half months, there is movement before then. Until the uterus has lifted out of the pelvic cavity into the abdomen, these movements are not felt because the wall of the uterus has no touch reception. It is only when it is lying against the abdomen that touch can be experienced. With very little gravitational pull from the earth, the fetus in the uterus is like a swimmer under water, or perhaps more like an astronaut in space. Movement is easy, and she twists and turns, flips from side to side, and while there is still room, before the eighth month of pregnancy, may somersault. She holds on to her umbilical cord, sometimes sucks her thumb, sometimes loses the thumb and darts her head from side to side searching for it again, bounces her head against the springy pelvic floor muscles when she has dropped deep into the pelvis, presses her feet against the thick muscle forming the top of the uterus in a stepping movement, rubs her eyes with tiny fists, and sometimes her whole body jerks with hiccups.

Some of these movements may occur in response to sound. The fetus hears from about the twenty-fifth week and may react strongly to loud noises and music, especially to the clash of cymbals or a brass band. At any time from about six weeks before term (the date the baby is expected) the fetus may drop lower into the pelvis and "engage." If it is a snug fit, it is then difficult for the fetus to make any big, whole-body movements, although he still kicks vigorously. The nature of the movements changes when this happens, unless the fetus is small and the mother's pelvis large, in which case he may stay equally active. The fetus who is lying with his back against his mother's spine may also feel very active, as the limbs are at the front.

It is important to be aware that there may be a qualitative difference in activity when the fetus engages in a vertex (head-down) position, facing the mother's side or back, however. If you do not know that this can happen, there may be panic when the movements are more restricted. Some women notice that their babies seem to sleep for longer periods then, too, rather as if the fetus is settled comfortably, like the dormouse in the teapot in *Alice in Wonderland*, and does not want to be disturbed. Perhaps it is a good time for conserving energy for labor.

"About a week before the expected date of arrival I thought William had died because he wasn't moving," Antonia says. "I became absolutely hysterical. I walked down a busy downtown street weeping. It took me three tries to get the nurse at the hospital to understand what I was saying, all my emotions were all over the place." She is a single mother and she felt submerged with loneliness: "I really needed someone to lean on then. Wow! Horrific! But the hospital said come up at once, and they put a monitor on the heart and he was just sleeping."

Because women can get alarmed about not feeling movements, some doctors think it is disturbing for them to be asked to note them. Some feel strongly that it is vital to reassure women at all cost and leave the worrying to the professionals. Doctors who believe this tend to favor tests that are done and analyzed at the hospital over anything that a woman can do herself.

Yet no one would suggest that a mother should leave observation of her baby solely to pediatricians once he is born. She is the one in day-to-day contact with her child and, as such, has more intimate knowledge than anyone who sees the child only for a clinical examination. Even when she does see a professional for advice, common sense tells us that the doctor ought to spend some time finding out what the mother knows about the child and listening to her. It is purely arbitrary to say that a mother should do this *after* birth, but that before the baby has emerged she need not bother herself with the matter and should "leave it to the doctor." While the baby is still inside her, in fact, there is closer contact between the two than they are ever going to experience after the birth.

A Kick Chart

One good way of checking that your baby is doing well in the uterus in the final weeks of pregnancy is to keep a kick chart, in which you count and record fetal movements. It is simple to do, noninvasive, and costs nothing, and can be very useful if induction is proposed for fetal compromise because it is thought that a baby is not doing well in utero, since you can probably produce evidence that your baby is vigorous. A baby who is moving well when she is awake (and remember that every baby has sleeping times) is *not at risk*. It is best to pick a regular time each day when you know from experience that your baby tends to be active. Most women find that this happens in the evening, when they have a chance to sit down and probably notice movements more readily than when busy and moving around. Antonia, remember, did not feel her baby move once while she was walking up and down the busy downtown street. If she had gone home and got into a bath or put her feet up on the bed she would have probably felt movements in the next hour or so.

Use graph paper, each square representing a half-hour period during your observation time. Shade in the square at which you feel the tenth movement each day. It should occur at approximately the same time each evening, give or take thirty minutes or so.

The result will be a chart that may look something like this:

June	Sat 1st	Sun 2nd	Mon 3rd	Tues 4th	Wed 5th	Thurs 6th	Fri 7th
5–5:30 p.m.							
5:30–6 p.m.				▬		▬	
6–6:30 p.m.	▬		▬		▬		▬
6:30–7 p.m.		▬					
7–7:30 p.m.							
7:30–8 p.m.							
8–8:30 p.m.							
8:30–9 p.m.							
9–9:30 p.m.							
9:30–10 p.m.							

That baby is doing well!

Just before being born the baby is likely to be a tight fit, so fetal movements may be reduced, and your chart may look like this:

June	Sat 8th	Sun 9th	Mon 10th	Tues 11th
5–5:30 p.m.				
5:30–6 p.m.				
6–6:30 p.m.	▬			
6:30–7 p.m.		▬		
7–7:30 p.m.			▬	
7:30–8 p.m.				▬

If at any time you have felt no fetal movement for a full twelve hours, call your obstetrician, the nurse at your doctor's office, or the hospital. There is no need to be alarmed, since the baby usually starts kicking soon after, but it is best to take action. One study of sixty-seven women who felt no fetal movements for at least twelve hours found that fifty-five of them had healthy babies after a labor that started normally.[2] The other twelve babies were passing meconium (the first contents of the bowel) or had abnormal heart rates, so labor was induced and all were born alive, ten in excellent condition and two with low Apgar ratings at five minutes (the Apgar score is a system of estimating the baby's condition at birth with reference to the heart rate, breathing, muscle tone, color, and response to stimulation). If you notice a 50 percent reduction in kicks continuing over several days, you should let the doctor know about it. You are your own best monitor of this, not because you are watching for danger but because you are in touch with your own baby and know your baby better than anyone else.

If the fetus is not moving, the doctor will probably decide to do a "nonstress test," described earlier. If the fetal heart rate does not increase with fetal movement, it is concluded that the baby is short of oxygen. If the baby starts kicking, it is a sign that all is well. If you know that your baby usually reacts to special kinds of music, you can try the effects of this even before you go to the hospital. One woman, a singer, said her baby always started moving when she was at a rehearsal or concert, so she could always check how he was by bursting into song! If you go past your due date, your observation of the baby's kicking is even more important, as careful recording could make all the difference between labor being induced and being able to start naturally. Kick charts done routinely by all women were not found to result in better outcomes than when done selectively, that is, only when a problem was suspected in the fetus.[3]

Every time you are seen in a prenatal appointment, the results are recorded in your medical chart by the nurse and the doctor or midwife. Results of the medical exam, including any lab work, subjects discussed, suggestions made, medications prescribed, etc., are recorded, too. You have the right to see your records if you wish. In the United States, women have a legal right to photocopies of their records. Although doctors sometimes think this may cause a patient unnecessary anxiety, since the information in the records is all about her body and her baby, it seems reasonable for a pregnant woman to have access to them.

In some systems of care, the midwives or doctors who provide your prenatal care will not attend your childbirth. Your chart containing records of all your appointments and tests will either be sent on to the hospital a few weeks before your due date, or you will be given a card with details of the results of examinations on it to take to the hospital with you. Otherwise, the only way you may see your records is if you ask to see them, or if they are handed to you to take into the consultation.

On the next two pages are some of the abbreviations you may find in your charts. Some appear with a question mark beside them. You will see that some abbreviations are similar to others. NAD (nothing abnormal detected) is a very common entry—don't confuse it with NTD (neural tube defect). If in any doubt about the writing, get up the courage to ask the person who wrote it.

THE CLINIC

AF	amniotic fluid
AFP	alpha-fetoprotein (see p. 47)
APH	antepartum hemorrhage
BP	blood pressure
BPD	biparietal diameter, head measurement. This is assessed by ultrasound, the usual method of recording fetal growth. It is most accurate before twenty-four weeks, widely inaccurate after thirty-four weeks. BPD grows 3.4mm a week at seventeen weeks, slows down to about a third of that at the end of pregnancy.
AROM	artificial rupture of membranes
CPD	cephalopelvic disproportion. The baby will not go through the mother's pelvis.
CST	contraction stress test
DPB	diastolic blood pressure (see p. 69)
E1, 2, or 3	estrogen output
EDD/EDC	estimated date of delivery/confinement
FBS	fetal blood sample
Fe	iron
FH/FHH	fetal heart heard
FHR	fetal heart rate
G	gravida (number of times pregnant)
GA	general anesthetic
GTT	glucose tolerance test, done if there is suspected diabetes
Hb	hemoglobin (see p. 71)
H/T	hypertension, high blood pressure
HVS	high vaginal swab
IUCD	intrauterine contraceptive device, loop or coil
IUD	intrauterine death
IUGR	intrauterine growth retardation
IUT	intrauterine transfusion, very rare
IV	intravenous
LMP	last menstrual period
CS	cesarean section
L/S	lecithin-sphingomyelin ratio, used to test maturity of fetal lungs, e.g., when mother has diabetes

MSU	midstream specimen of urine
NAD	nothing abnormal detected
NTD	neural tube defect
OA	occiput anterior, baby lying head down, facing mother's back. Most favorable position.
LOA	left occiput anterior
ROA	right occiput anterior
OCT	oxytocin challenge test. Intravenous infusion of oxytocin while monitoring fetal heart to see how baby responds to strong contractions.
OP	occiput posterior. Baby lying head down, facing mother's front. Expect long first stage of labor, with backache. Keep upright and moving, if possible.
LOP	left occiput posterior
ROP	right occiput posterior
OT	occiput transverse. Baby lying head down, the side of its head toward mother's front. May move to anterior or posterior.
P	para (number of births of viable children)
PE_2/PGE_2	prostaglandin used in induction
PET	preeclamptic toxemia (see p. 70)
PPH	postpartum hemorrhage
RE	rectal examination
POP	persistent occiput posterior
SBP	systolic blood pressure (see p. 69)
SVD	spontaneous vaginal delivery/spontaneous vertex delivery
T,R	test of thyroid function
US	ultrasound
VE	vaginal examination

5

Doctors

One great advantage in being older and more experienced in coping with people can be that a woman is more skilled and confident when it comes to finding out what she needs to know about the medical system, maneuvering her way through it, and getting what she wants. This may have to start when the pregnancy is first confirmed. One woman, very happy to be pregnant by a man with whom she had lived for two years, went to a gynecologist to make sure that all was well. He told her she was definitely pregnant and then said, "When do you want the abortion?" "Abortion?" she said. "I want this baby." "Oh," he replied, "forty and unmarried. Most unusual." She found she had to convince the doctor that she wanted to go ahead with the pregnancy, an experience that might have thrown a younger woman.

The woman in her thirties or forties is more likely to know where to go to get accurate information, how to sift the evidence, and how to negotiate the kind of childbirth she would like to have, in the setting of her choice. Julie was having her fourth baby at forty. The others had all been born at home, and she wanted this one at home, too. "I merely told them that unless there were pressing medical contraindications, I would stay at home. One said that they might not have a midwife available. I said that didn't deter me." He said no more and a midwife duly appeared. "I did need to have a certain amount of toughness," she added. Another woman had fully intended to have her baby in the hospital, but one week before her due date she visited the delivery room to look around. She decided then and there that she was not prepared to have her baby in such surroundings. So she had a home birth.

After a four-hour wait at the clinic, Caroline was told by a junior doctor that she was to be induced. He said that she would need an epidural because induced labor was always more painful and a first labor would last at least twenty-four hours. He told her that she must make up her mind about this immediately. When she arrived home weeping and distressed, John, her partner, took immediate action and phoned the senior obstetrician to find out exactly what was happening, and why. Caroline was persuaded by what he said that induction was the best course of action.

The induction went well, and she needed no painkillers at all. She asked for an epidural just as she was entering transition, but on learning that she was almost fully dilated decided it was not necessary. "The anesthetist came back to give me 'just a little jab to help the pain.' John asked what was in this 'jab,' and the anesthetist said, 'a narcotic, Pethidine (Demerol).' We said, 'No thank you.' " The baby slipped out shortly thereafter, and Caroline was delighted to have had a spontaneous birth without any drugs. Her partner had been her ally and support in this. "Together we had done it." Summing up, she says, "The process of labor and giving birth was highly satisfactory, partly I'm sure due to the fact that we asserted our rights and developed a very positive relationship with the midwife."

In fact, for most women it is not as straightforward as that. Many say they find that doctor's appointments are dreadful, communication is inadequate, and doctors' assumptions that patients should have a passive role leave them feeling frustrated and helpless. Carole lives in an industrial town and had shared care between midwives and doctors. She contrasts the midwives' clinic, where it is easy to discuss worries and ask questions, with the physicians' clinic, where women sit for long periods and "never see the same person twice." In fact, she says she once sat there for two and a half hours. "The doctor puts in an appearance, says, 'Good afternoon, is everything all right . . . I'll just listen to your tummy . . . Thank you, see you next week.'" She never managed to extract any information about her pregnancy from the obstetrician, but nevertheless continued to attend the clinic to undergo this ritual.

Another woman, who might be considered competent in communication since she is a postdoctoral developmental psychologist engaged in research, says that she had to "squeeze every single piece of information" out of the doctor and was "appalled at the whole business." Joan refused to go to the hospital clinic after being "treated like a moron" and had appointments with her family doctor instead. Dorothy, having her third baby at forty, insisted on a home birth after her experience at the prenatal clinic:

> I was handed a booklet urging me to bring any worries to the doctor. When I am ushered in to him he addresses his questions to me with his back turned while filling in my form. He turns only to look at my bulge and my vulva and never addresses any remarks to my face at all. At what point does one break in with one's inmost anxieties? Perhaps I should have gone in a frog mask just to see if he would notice?

Feeling Old

Many women are pleasantly surprised to find that they are not alone in being older mothers and that what one woman called "obstetric geriatrics" are becoming commonplace. Clinic staff, however, may, often inadvertently, suggest that pregnancy and labor are going to be especially difficult. One expectant mother of thirty-seven said that throughout her pregnancy she felt that the famous teaching hospital she attended treated her as "a freak."

Nancy, age thirty-six, said that she was trying to find out at the hospital whether she could arrange a water birth and have an eight-hour discharge. They told her to speak to the head nurse to find out about hospital policy. The appointment for which she asked was long delayed, so she asked the obstetrician during her next prenatal visit. He said, "Oh, I wouldn't worry about all that if I were you. At your age you are more than likely to spend the last few weeks in the hospital and then to be induced or have a cesarean."

The woman who is having a late baby after a long gap is able to compare the present experience with previous births. If her first children are already in their late teens, she spans the time during which there has been a complete medicalization of childbirth. One woman, for example, commented on the contrast between the personal care she was given when she was twenty and felt "rather clever" at having a baby and the impersonal, factory-farm baby production she experienced when she had another baby at forty-two, and remarked how "grim" it is nowadays. Another said: "Pregnancy and childbirth seem to be a nightmare now. People are very afraid and forever worrying about their due date and whether the baby is growing." Several women had such bad experiences with big hospitals when they started second families in their late thirties that they insisted on having subsequent babies in a birth center or at home and were very glad they did. Some had first babies at home. They often found they had to battle for this, though occasionally it was welcomed by the physician. Jill, age thirty-three, said she went to the doctor "armed with statistics and arguments about the desirability of a home birth . . . whereupon he took all the wind out of my sails by saying, 'Oh, yes, that'll be rather nice. I haven't done one of those for a long time.' " The hospital doctors were a different matter. One made it clear to Jill that "the decision about where to have my baby had nothing to do with me and would be made on my behalf by her. I soon disabused her of that notion and amended the relevant parts she marked on my chart." It is not just that hospital care is sometimes stark and unfriendly; many women feel that the failure to achieve any continuity actually results in second-class or dangerous medicine and obstetrics.

The pregnant woman has a responsibility, for herself and her baby, to discover the choices open to her, weigh their relative advantages, and make sure that everyone knows what she wants. It means that she also has to be sufficiently courageous to complain when necessary and to withdraw her consent for procedures that she is not happy about, unless more convincing arguments are produced. This is very different from the traditional feminine role, and many women feel acutely uncomfortable with it. They want to please; it feels good to make the doctor smile; they do not want to fuss, or, indeed, to be noticed as different in any way. It is much easier to conform to the doctor's expectations of the "good patient." Diana Scully, in her study of the training of obstetricians and gynecologists in the United States, asked doctors how they would describe a good patient.[1] Their answers emphasized passivity, obedience, and middle-class status. One said: "The main thing is that the patient understands what I say, listens to what I say, does what I say, believes what I say."

The "Vocal Minority"

A woman who has had the opportunity of education and a career has special responsibilities in this because she is speaking for other women who have not had her advantages and who may be even more confused and anxious than she is. Yet she has to be prepared for possible hostility or suspicion on the part of the doctor simply *because* she is an educated woman asking questions (in the past, the medical press has sometimes labeled such women the "vocal minority"). A doctor has often been trained to see pregnant women only as patients who receive instructions and may think of skills of communication as giving these instructions clearly, rather than as a two-way conversation. If the patient does not comply, she is "a defaulter."

Ann Oakley, in her book *Subject Women*, writes:

The idea that it is *women* who cause the deaths of babies—by not going [for prenatal care] (or not going early enough), by smoking, eating the wrong food, having sexual intercourse, not being married . . . implicitly acknowledges women's disobedience in doing what *they* think is best for themselves and their babies.[2]

So it is often difficult to talk with doctors and get them to listen to you. Few doctors today would openly state, as did one in the 1970s to a patient who questioned his diagnosis, "I will tell you what is wrong with you, I will tell you what your symptoms are, and I will tell you what to do. I am the doctor and you will kindly not forget the fact."[3] But there are probably many doctors who come very near such an outburst, especially when a pregnant woman is insistent about the kind of care she would like, and how she wants the birth to be.

In a footnote, Oakley adds that articles published by Oliver and Louise Gillie in *The Sunday Times* of London were often referred to by doctors, in consultations she was observing in a hospital, with women who queried their treatment, as improper sources of information. Any woman who questions treatment on the basis of something she has read may be dismissed with "You mustn't believe everything you read" or castigated with the shocked discovery "You've been reading *books*!"

There are, of course, universities where psychology and the acquisition of interview techniques form part of medical courses. But even there these skills may be seen as means of acquiring power over patients and manipulating them effectively. A professor of obstetrics, describing the advances in the teaching of medical students in his own department, told me, "We have a film on how to deal with a difficult patient." (We are still awaiting, unfortunately, the film on how to deal with a difficult doctor.) He went on to explain some of the techniques of interviewing that were taught: "Eye contact is important," he said, and fixing me with an unwavering glare, added, "You will notice that I am making eye contact with *you* now."

Doctors now also learn to see pregnant women as "consumers," and to take patient satisfaction under consideration. According to this paradigm, pregnant women are like shoppers allowed to choose between brands of laundry detergent or select cakes in a well-presented display. But suppose they do not want cakes in the first place? It is the duty of the store manager to see that they do.

Women are not just consumers of health care. In childbirth we are the producers, without whom doctors would have no jobs. Women should be able to say what they want, and—unless it can be shown, through properly conducted research, that this is positively dangerous—expect it to be provided.

It is not only a question of expressing feelings. It is often claimed that all pregnant women are emotionally vulnerable. Perhaps. But this is no excuse for treating women as incapable of rational thought, or so concerned with their own emotions that they are "selfish and egotistical," and cannot be trusted to consider their babies' needs.[4] The opposite is nearer the truth. Women who want loving people around them in labor, who criticize excessive intervention in childbirth, or decline drugs, those who seek home birth or water birth, or who insist that they are not separated from their newborn babies do these things *because* they want what is best for their babies, are concerned about their babies' safety and well-being, and are thinking about how they would like to welcome them into the world.

Being "High Risk"

As we have seen, the older woman may find that she is in a "high-risk" category simply because of her age. For some obstetricians this classification includes all first-time mothers over thirty. Others tend to include in this category only women of thirty-five and older. A few believe that it should include women having first babies at twenty-eight. Different terms are used to describe the women. "Elderly primigravida" is one, which, as one woman said, "made me feel very long in the tooth." A woman who was five feet tall was very alarmed at being categorized as an "elderly *dwarf* primigravida." A "gravida" is simply a pregnant woman. So a "multigravida" is one who has had previous pregnancies. If you are pregnant but have had two miscarriages you are a "gravida"! The other term is "parity" to describe the number of previous pregnancies which have gone through to twenty-eight weeks or after. If you are "para 3" you have had three births. If you are "para 3 + 1" you have had three births and one miscarriage. Multiple births and miscarriages are counted as one in this system of reckoning. A "nulliparous" woman is one who is having her first pregnancy, though the terms "primagravida" or "primipara" are often used loosely instead.

There is no reason to think that birth will be more painful or difficult because you are over thirty-five. Many women in their late thirties and forties are healthier than they have ever been because they care for themselves, understand their bodies, and ensure that they get exercise and have a good diet. A healthy woman of forty is in much better condition for labor than an unhealthy one in her twenties.

It may also be that a woman has more stamina and courage than when she was younger. An experienced midwife, Ina May Gaskin, says that women over thirty-five are unlikely to "waste time and precious energy during labor by feeling sorry for themselves or by fighting labor." She claims that "a woman with a mature attitude is usually able to use the energy of labor efficiently, to rest effectively while dilating or in between pushes." She thinks it is ridiculous to consider entire categories of women at high-risk simply because of their age and accuses doctors of "a very crude and unscientific brand of obstetrics."[5]

Perinatal Mortality

Statistically, risks to the baby are higher to women giving birth over thirty-five than for those in their twenties. Under twenty the risks are also higher. The perinatal mortality rate (PMR) is a record of deaths of babies at birth or in the week following. The figure is given as a proportion of 1000 births. In the United States, the PMR is now about 12 per 1000. This is a crude figure, however, because it does not tell us anything about the quality of life of the babies who live or about the mothers who are most likely to have babies who live or about those who are most likely to have babies who die. Age is only one factor associated with perinatal mortality. It is clear that perinatal mortality reflects poverty. It stems from all the things we associate with social disadvantage: lack of education, poor housing, overcrowding, inadequate nutrition, stress, environmental poisons, and perhaps also simply from not being able to operate in "the system"—being powerless and unable even to claim social security benefits.

It is difficult to isolate these variables because being poor brings with it many other disadvantages for the fetus. Smoking in pregnancy is more common. Some eight deaths of every thousand births might be avoided if women did not smoke when pregnant, and many more babies would arrive with better birth weights. Congenital malformations such as spina bifida, including those that are incompatible with life, are also more frequent at the bottom of the social scale, and these alone account for 22 percent of perinatal deaths. Seventy percent of babies who die do so because they are born prematurely. Here again there is an association with social class. The higher the social class, the lower the percentage of preterm births. The poor may live in heavily built-up inner-city areas, where lead from car exhausts pollutes the air. If a woman is at the bottom of the social scale she is more likely to get pregnant while still in her teens, and some women who cannot cope with contraception or whose partners are unwilling to, go on having babies when they are themselves in poor health. There is also a continuum of disadvantages; although individuals break out of the pattern, it tends to be passed on from parents to children. There is mounting evidence that it is important that a woman have good nutrition, not only during pregnancy, but before. This reflects the social-class culture in which she lives and perhaps also that in which she was reared. Her nutrition while she was growing up may be another factor in the equation, and perhaps even her own parents' nutrition.

The upshot of all this is that if you are reading this page, the statistics of highest risk, stemming from poor social conditions, do not apply to you. If you are willing to terminate a pregnancy if fetal disability is diagnosed, any risk is still further reduced. In good health yourself and with a straightforward pregnancy in which no special risk factors are detected, you can expect a normal labor and a healthy baby. No one can guarantee this, but generalizations that older mothers always have difficult births, that an older woman's baby after a normal pregnancy is at greater risk, or that older mothers are less successful at breast-feeding are all untrue.

It is difficult to measure pain or guess whether the birth is likely to be more (or less) painful because of your age, because so much depends on your attitude and whether you feel that pain is *attacking* you or working *for* you. This in itself is influenced by the environment in which birth takes place, by psychological factors such as whether or not you feel cherished and emotionally supported, and by such things as tiredness or exhaustion and conflicting emotions about what is happening. All these affect the perception of pain. One woman, who actually delivered in the bathtub at home, comfortably lapped in warm water, commented: "I do not want to give the impression that it was all dreamlike pleasure. Obviously if it had not been for the birth of our baby, the same sensations would have been painful. Only the love and the joy transformed the contractions into a 'labor' rather than a 'pain.' "

Induced Labor

Some obstetricians have a policy of inducing labor—that is, starting it artificially—in all their patients over a certain age. A doctor will sometimes tell the woman in early pregnancy, "I won't let you go past your due date at your age" or tell her to come into the hospital a week or two weeks *before* she is due, to be induced. Unless you have a *medical* condition, the most common of which is diabetes (not *pregnancy* diabetes, which is different), which means that labor may be started early, an obstetrician cannot possibly tell whether you can be induced with safety to your baby while you are still in the first half of pregnancy. Even with modern methods of estimating gestation such as serial ultrasound, mistakes can be made about the age of the fetus, and occasionally babies are delivered before they are ready for life, with consequent breathing problems.

The length of pregnancy is assumed to be 280 days or forty weeks, often regardless of the length of the menstrual cycle. When periods have been irregular it is especially difficult to know when ovulation occurred. Thirty percent of babies are delivered before the estimated date and 70 percent after that date. Most pregnancies last anywhere between thirty-eight and forty-two weeks, though 90 percent of births take place within 10 days of the due date. Your age is an insufficient reason for inducing labor.

Induction should be performed only after you have discussed

the reasons for it, had time to think about it, been told exactly what happens, and given your consent. It is easier for you to consider the matter if you are out of the hospital, in your normal surroundings. Some doctors expect patients to agree on the spot, or else send them into an adjoining room for a few minutes to make up their minds. You can say, "I'd like more time to think about this, and I don't think I can let you know before next Tuesday," or "I want time to talk this over with my partner," although the doctor may then ask, "Is your partner an obstetrician?" and if you say no, say, "Well, how can he possibly help you decide, then?" (which is what happened to one woman of thirty-six).

Your childbirth educator may be a good person with whom to discuss possible induction. She knows what happens and will probably also know which obstetricians perform it most readily, and if they tend to pressure their patients into it or frequently suggest that the baby will die if the induction does not go ahead. Some obstetricians regularly subject their patients to a form of emotional blackmail. Women say that they are asked, "Are you prepared to accept responsibility if your baby dies?" or "You do realize you are risking your baby's life, do you?"

Induction can be carried out in several ways: inserting prostaglandin gel in or around your cervix to ripen it, waiting a few hours and repeating it; breaking your bag of waters (amniotomy); giving you an intravenous drip of Pitocin (oxytocin); or any two or three of these combined.

If an expectant mother tries to discuss episiotomy, a cut made to enlarge the birth outlet, some obstetricians may make her feel accused of deliberately intending to injure her baby by making the birth difficult for it, and threatened with postnatal sexual problems and the consequent breakdown of a sexual relationship, and by prolapse later in life unless she agrees to one.[6] These obstetricians genuinely believe that their way is better than nature's and can offer improved and, what Sir John Dewhurst, former President of the Royal College of Gynecologists and Obstetricians in Britain, calls "enhanced" childbirth. They are sincere and often deeply committed to their beliefs. When you discuss your treatment with them, bear this in mind. Also be aware that numerous research studies do not confirm the belief that episiotomy is beneficial.

Though it may be taken for granted that an older woman needs an episiotomy, understanding of the way a woman's body functions in childbirth and support from her attendants to push spontaneously, without commands or coaxing, only as much as and when *she* wants to, often enables her to give birth without one. It is no wonder that women tear or require an episiotomy when they are urged to hold their breath and ordered to push as long and as hard as they are able. Under these conditions even emptying our bowels would also be painful and traumatic. Moreover, lying or sitting positions put more strain on the perineum. Side-lying or upright positions, such as crouching, kneeling, squatting forward, standing, or being on all fours, all reduce stress on the perineum and distribute pressure more evenly on the tissues surrounding the vagina.

If it is your first baby, the second stage may take longer than it would have when you were younger because the head needs to press down gradually through layers of tissue, opening them out rather like a fan-pleated skirt, and it is the first time you will have opened up this wide. It is often assumed that a first-time older mother has tissues that are inflexible, without the "give" of younger tissues. But there have been no studies published on this, and since we know that tissue flexibility is affected by general health and by diet, it may be that an older woman in good health and on a balanced diet can have tissues that are in better condition than those of a younger woman in poor health who keeps going on "junk" food. An older woman who pays particular attention to perineal well-being, with pelvic-floor exercises performed not just at exercise sessions but as movements throughout the day, and who, perhaps, also uses oil to massage her perineum regularly and help her get the feeling of "giving," is preparing herself in the best way for delivery without the need of episiotomy. Since this operation is performed routinely by many physicians, however, it is important to speak to your doctor about it in advance. Tell him that you want to deliver without episiotomy, if possible, and ask him to help you achieve this.

Although your childbirth educator can probably give you information, she is usually torn between giving you facts so that you can decide for yourself and making things as easy and comfortable as possible for you so that whatever happens you are able to adapt to labor. She may say to herself, "If this woman is going to have an induced labor anyway, I can help her accept it psychologically and reassure her about what happens." And she is quite right if she tells you that some women have very happy, straightforward induced labors. On the other hand, many do not. Although techniques of induction have improved in most hospitals since 1978, the date of my own study of women's experiences of induction, research then revealed that women being induced needed far more painkillers.[7] Ninety-five percent of women who had attended National Childbirth Trust prenatal classes had drugs for pain relief when labor was induced. Women who go to classes often hope to manage without drugs as far as possible. When labor was not induced, fifty percent of women managed without them. Those women who had already had babies with a noninduced labor were asked to compare the induced labor with the previous labor which was not induced. Usually second births are easier than the first. The majority of these women said that the second birth was *more* painful.

The babies did not do so well either, though more babies of induced labors were probably at risk for other reasons. A much larger proportion of newborns were separated from their mothers because they were put in the intensive care nursery. These babies were unlikely all to have been ill, since policy used to be to put every baby delivered after a difficult labor under the watchful eyes of the intensive care nurse just in case. Since the publication of the work of Klaus and Kennell on bonding, this policy has been changed in many hospitals.[8]

Because of the analgesics the mothers had taken, there was also another kind of separation. Many women experienced a pharmacological separation from their babies, whom they could not hold because they felt too "woozy" or could not see because they fell asleep. This separation severely affected the first meeting between mother and baby immediately following birth and for several hours afterward. It also affected breast-feeding, since the time when the baby can most naturally and easily go to the mother's breast after birth was missed. Many of the babies were knocked out by the drugs the mother had taken. This was usually Demerol or Demerol in combination with other drugs.

Once labor is induced and the bag of waters has been ruptured, there is no turning back. The obstetrician is committed to getting you delivered within twenty-four hours. To wait any longer than this increases the risk of infection. He has to be prepared, therefore, to engage in "active management" to keep to a timetable. Professor Ian Donald warns that "any intervention, however apparently trivial, carries with it the responsibilities for consequences . . ."[9] The decision to induce labor is as serious a one as a decision to perform a cesarean section. The rate of intravenous oxytocin can be stepped up to make the uterus work harder. This may cause more pain, so a narcotic or an epidural may be offered before this is done. If the cervix fails to dilate quickly or the baby reacts with type two dips in its heart rate (a slowing of the baby's heart after the end of a contraction), ones that persist after the contraction has ended, the obstetrician will be ready to intervene with cesarean section. If the cervix dilates but there is a holdup then, because the woman has an epidural and cannot feel how to push, or is too doped or exhausted to do so, delivery can be accomplished by forceps, or sometimes by vacuum extractor. Induced labors are more likely to finish with forceps[10] or cesarean[11] deliveries.

Failed Induction

An induction that ends in a cesarean section is a *failed* induction. Two percent upward of all inductions end in a cesarean. Professor

Donald warned: "No method of induction is both absolutely certain and safe."[12] In Britain induction was most in vogue in the early 1970s. Then nearly 40 percent of all labors were induced. The rate has fallen steadily since then, largely because it has been discovered that high induction rates do not save babies' lives. But there is still wide variation among different hospitals and even inside the same hospital among different physicians. You can ask the obstetrician the induction rate in his hospital. If it is below about 15 percent, listen with great care to his explanation of why you need to be induced because he will have good reasons. If it is over 25 percent, some labors are probably being induced unnecessarily. Between these two figures there is a gray area, because hospitals in different cities care for women from widely varying backgrounds, and high-risk women from poor social backgrounds *may* benefit from more intervention than women who have no known risk factors. In fact, studies reveal that poor women get *less* intervention than women who are better off."[13]

It is widely believed that since the induction "scare" of the 1970s induction rates have plummeted. This is not so. Even where fewer inductions are done, acceleration of labors that have already started is common. This practice, too, has its risks, which are much the same as those of induction. Some obstetricians believe that it is right to manage actively the labors of all first-time mothers over thirty or thirty-five. It is more difficult to resist an intravenous drip of synthetic oxytocin once you are already in the hospital and in bed. But no intervention should take place unless you have it explained to you and you have agreed to it. In practice, once a patient has been told about a procedure in however rudimentary a way—"I'm going to give you a bit of help now" or "I'm just going to give you a little prick" (one woman, usually refined, exclaimed, "I don't care whether your prick is big or little. I don't want it!") —it is taken that she has understood and accepted the intervention. So you have to be quick to say, "No, thank you" or "Hold on! I'd like to discuss this."

Induction should be done in only two cases: when the baby is obviously safer out than in because the intrauterine environment is poor; and when the mother's health is going to suffer severely if the pregnancy continues. The cervix should be ripe. If it is not, in some countries a failed induction is quite likely. Measures used to ripen the cervix include nipple stimulation for several days and, in some centers, prostaglandin suppositories placed in the cervix. The latter technique is being used experimentally in the United States and is in wide use in Britain. Sometimes oxytocin is unnecessary, as labor proceeds with prostaglandin or breast stimulation alone. This is much more comfortable for the mother and may allow labor to progress more normally because she can be up and about.

If you are induced, do not expect labor to be rapid. It can be long and drawn-out, and the so-called latent phase before there is effective dilation of the cervix may be prolonged.

Similarly, if a cesarean section is recommended, although the news comes as a shock, take time to discuss the pros and cons with your doctor. It may be that a trial of labor, with everything ready for a cesarean section if necessary, is a better idea. In many cases no one knows for sure what a uterus can do until contractions have gotten under way. If it proves to be a cesarean after all, consider the possibility of one with epidural anesthesia. This enables you to be awake when your baby is born and aware of everything that is going on. Abby, a new mother, said it was "fantastic!"

> They erected a green curtain across my tummy so I couldn't see. I felt no pain, only pressure. Then as soon as they delivered the baby they lowered the curtain and gave her to me. I fell in love with her right away. We were lost in wonder over our new daughter.

Fathers are often present at a cesarean under epidural, and this is worth asking for. If an obstetrician has not had a father there before, he may find it helpful and reassuring to meet your partner beforehand and may be willing to try it as an experiment with someone he already knows.

Self-Doubt

Seeds of self-doubt are sometimes sown inadvertently in an older woman's mind during pregnancy by other people's remarks. You laugh them off at the time, but in the middle of the night they sprout. One woman of thirty-eight said that pregnant teenagers in the hospital were "aghast" when they learned her age and exclaimed, "You're old enough to be my mother!" and "My God! You never imagine *teachers* having *babies*!" Older mothers often mention remarks made by doctors like "You're a bit old for this sort of thing, aren't you?" or "We'll have to keep an eye on you." One woman was lying on the examination table with her lower half exposed when the senior obstetrician swept in, followed by a retinue of students, notebooks poised. "Ah," exclaimed the great man, "here we have the perfect example of an elderly primigravida!" "And a *talking* elderly primigravida, too!" said the patient, raising her head.

In spite of feeling vulnerable and at a disadvantage with her underwear off, an older woman really does have more of a chance of getting the doors of communication open with the doctors, even if they often need a bit of a shove. She may be of the same age as those caring for her, so they have that in common, or the doctor may be younger so that she does not feel in awe of him.

A sense of humor helps, if only because the woman who insists on knowing what is to be done to her and why is readily labeled as "anxious," "neurotic," or "difficult," and this may be written into her chart. If you can be firm and persistent but at the same time keep a light touch, you give yourself more chance of genuine "rapport." If you have a male partner, taking him with you to meet the obstetrician means that he not only appreciates what you go through at your prenatal visits but can ask questions, too. It may also put the obstetrician more at ease, as some hospital doctors do not like talking to women and find it much simpler to talk "man to man." If you do this, you have to be sure that the two will not start colluding together, however, and making decisions *for* you. Get as much information as you can, talk through together in ad-

Think of your doctor in his pajamas

vance the things that matter most to you, and make notes of priorities. You might even try acting out a hypothetical discussion, taking turns playing the part of the obstetrician. If the answer to a question is unconvincing, how are you going to follow it up? Remember that you do not have to come to any snap decisions. Unless there is a dire emergency, you can always take time to think things through. Just say, "I'd like time to think about that."

Talk with your doctor as a human being, not as an authoritarian professional in a white coat. (Think of him in his pajamas.) And bear in mind that many obstetricians are rushed, overworked, and under great pressure, because they see far too many patients in too short a time. This does not mean that you should not take time to talk because you are aware of the other patients waiting (though that is a natural reaction) but that you think ahead to what you want to say, use the interview constructively, and *thank* him for giving the time. Sheer pressure of numbers sometimes means that you have to put off a discussion until another time. Some doctors spend on average only two minutes with each patient. Explain that this discussion is important to you and make at least an unofficial appointment for it. If you cannot get anyone to make time for you, write a letter to the obstetrician. Once something is in your chart it tends to be noticed, if only because it is open to other people's perusal, too.

A woman may choose a woman doctor—one who has had babies herself—because she thinks it will be easier to talk to her. Some women obstetricians understand just how disempowering the medical system can be for childbearing women because they have experienced this themselves and have not become sucked into the medical establishment. But you cannot assume that because your doctor is a woman, she shares any of your views about birth. Women in obstetrics have to struggle for recognition and status against a system that is heavily dominated by men. To do this, they often copy men. It may be the only route to success in their careers.

Some of the problems older mothers encounter in pregnancy and labor result from the obstetrician's concern about them and from too much doctoring rather than from any inherent condition. Pregnancy is seen primarily not as a natural physiological state but as a hazardous process. Judith Lumley, a lecturer in obstetrics in Australia, puts it this way:

> The distinction between normal and abnormal pregnancy has become blurred. Some doctors reject the "normal" as inappropriate, and classify all pregnant women as low risk, medium risk or high risk patients. Normality becomes an accolade, to be bestowed after the event on the few women who pass through pregnancy and birth without deviating from the physiological ideal at any point.[14]

In this, the older pregnant woman, especially one having a baby for the first time, has all the odds stacked against her. Obstetric and midwifery textbooks sometimes discuss her as if she had one foot in the grave, with increased chances of uterine fibroids, miscarriage, hypertension, premature labor, long, dysfunctional labor, forceps delivery, and cesarean section. It is understandable that the doctor who does not have much experience of the normal, healthy older pregnant woman may become anxious and then convey this anxiety to his patient. When a woman's blood pressure goes up, for example, this may be a direct result of a proliferation of investigations that threaten confidence, warnings from doctors, and stressful prenatal appointments. The woman goes in feeling happy and fit and comes out feeling reproductively incompetent and sick with fear, frustration, and, often, suppressed anger. It would be surprising if this did *not* have an effect on her blood pressure.

Keeping Calm

It may help to build some calm into your daily life: yoga, meditation, relaxation or a time for slow full breathing, or simply luxuriating in a leisurely bath in a darkened room. Finding a way to express what you feel is also vital. Anger is legitimate, and it can help to cry, shout, or punch pillows. Most women try to go on as if nothing had happened and to be "reasonable," thus giving implicit acceptance to the assumption that anything can be required of a woman *for the sake of her baby*. Objecting to the way you are being treated can seem selfish since it is all being done for your baby.

A thirty-eight-year-old woman who is herself a midwife came to realize halfway through her pregnancy that she wanted a home birth: "I felt, 'I can't leave this house. I need to give birth in my own space.' I told my doctor, who was horrified. She upset me a lot. She told me that the baby would die. She was totally uncooperative, but two of my best friends are the best midwives around —so I simply bypassed her."

When things go wrong, a doctor lacks any understanding of your experience, there are failures in communication, or care becomes abusive, write to complain both to the doctor concerned and to the relevant authority. A woman who had the Triple Test was informed that she had a one in seventy chance of a Down's syndrome baby. Her doctor, rather than discussing with her arrangements for amniocentesis, took it for granted that she would have an abortion, and booked a hospital bed for it. When the woman said that she did not plan on having an abortion, the doctor replied, "Oh, well, Down's syndrome children can be very affectionate—like dogs."

Some older women have relatively good experiences of care, especially those who have careers in the health services. They feel they are on familiar ground and may know those caring for them. Others enjoy being part of the workings of an efficiently run institution and feel secure and confident with the application of modern technology to the business of childbirth. Fran says that her "present idea of heaven would be to spend a week in the hospital, *enjoying* anonymity, gloriously free from domestic demands and the company of my (albeit loving) family." With a sideswipe at my own views, she adds: "Some women are not thrown into hysteria at the sight of gleaming machinery." Even she, however, describes one incident in her happy hospital experience in which she felt completely depersonalized. She had been pushed out of the delivery room on a gurney and was going up to the ward in an elevator, surrounded by porters and nurses:

> They were joking about their weekend dates, and I wondered if it would be rude to join in the conversation. But it became clear to me that it wasn't expected. I was simply a body in transit.

It takes an effort of will and imagination to move on from that situation to accept that caregivers can be collaborators rather than powerful authority figures appropriating from us the responsibility for the outcome of the pregnancy. Although a distorted medical perspective often implies that statistics ought to rule our lives, personal experience tells us that such views of life are untenable. The value we attach to particular events and qualities of relationships must also affect the decisions we make. If we thought only in terms of statistics and of reducing the perinatal mortality by one more decimal point, no matter what effect this had on human emotions and values, we could make it a matter of public policy to detect all multiple pregnancies by ultrasound and abort them immediately since these babies are likely to be born preterm and be of low birth weight. That we do not abort all twins and triplets shows that values do not depend on mere arithmetic. Even doctors most passionately concerned about perinatal mortality statistics have not proposed this solution. Nor can we ever have *complete* safety in childbirth. Expecting a baby to be perfect if you do all the right things and have every available investigation sets an impossibly high and unrealistic standard. As more and more tests for fetal well-being are developed, a situation may develop in which the older expectant mother could spend much of her time undergoing investigative procedures of one kind or another. The decision as to how much to probe and investigate is not a medical matter in the long run, but has to do with the quality of life and how much intervention we are prepared to tolerate for the sake of more knowledge. The pursuit of perfection in human reproduction is a mirage.

Ross Mitchell of the Department of Child Health at Dundee University expresses it this way:

In human reproduction, the analogy of the production line or conveyor belt is inappropriate: it implies a uniform, repeatable, and flawless standard of product, anything less than this being instantly and rightly rejected. In laying too great emphasis on the goal of faultless excellence, we may have done a misservice to some children and their parents. Every person is the result of many interacting influences, some beneficial and others inimical to development. The mother's anxious scrutiny of her new baby to assure herself that he is unblemished and her overreaction to the slightest deviation from an ideal norm are intensified by the tacit professional assumption that perfection is the yardstick.[15]

6

Life After the
Baby Comes

When you are still pregnant it is very difficult to summon the imaginative energy to think about how things may be after the baby comes. Discussions about how you might feel, for instance, seem purely academic. The birth is the all-important challenge. Yet for many women, that fourth trimester of pregnancy, the three months after the birth, its delights and difficulties, are more exciting, exhausting, and deeply satisfying than even the birth itself. You are rudely awakened from a peak emotional experience straight into an activity and commitment that keeps you at full speed almost twenty-four hours of every day. First-time older mothers say:

> The most devastating thing is that once the child is born it is a total stranger. You have some idea of the times it will wake and sleep from the times it has been kicking you to bits, but otherwise you know nothing about it. This is frightening.
>
> I felt I was a feeding and changing machine. The constant physical and emotional involvement with a dependent small human

being was such a contrast to my previous life (as a librarian in an academic library). I realized how unprepared I was. Watching a public health nurse bathe a doll is a far cry from the real thing.

❧

I had awful depression on the third day. Difficult because Robert (my husband) was still physically and emotionally exhausted. He's not used to feeling so much so intensely. We yelled at each other and I cried and wanted to die—about what we're going to eat for dinner, for goodness sake! The midwife was worried and asked her relief to come in next day—to find me up and about singing and washing diapers.

❧

Having been a teacher used to dealing with about thirty-five children, I thought I'd find a baby a piece of cake. Although I was on a "high," I still found those first six weeks totally exhausting. I fell in love with my daughter from the first second I saw her. It really was like being in love. Every time I woke up I'd be overwhelmed with excitement, yes, even at three in the morning, I loved being with her, near her, touching her, kissing her, looking at her, and thinking constantly of her.

The responsibility for this new life can be frightening. A woman who has been anxiously trying to fit the whole business of having a baby and rearing him into her own well-organized lifestyle may sometimes feel as if the ground has opened beneath her. The conflict between her career goals, her wants and the demands of her own ego, and the overwhelming pull of the baby's needs may produce grotesque and disturbing fantasies, both nighttime dreams and daytime mind-images that have the quality of hallucinations. A woman who had taken steps to be sterilized before she decided she wanted to have a baby was deeply troubled by the sense of her power to avoid pregnancy. It was as if she were the bad queen or the wicked witch of the story books:

Every night since I came home from the hospital I have woken up not knowing where she is, thinking that she's in the bed, or believing that she's been squashed or suffocated. Sometimes the disturbance is quite mild and John tells me that she's in her room. At the other extreme, I have woken up crying out and desperately searching for her under the pillows.

There is also the astonishing reality of the baby, not just a package but a person. Many women feel the wave of passionate love that enthralls them is so intense that it makes it difficult to cope in the "real" world, with its lunch and supper times, daily routines, dealing with visitors, the questions people ask, and the demands of other human relations and people's expectations of you. Sylvia Plath vividly suggests the strength of this complete giving of one-self to the baby in her poem "Three Women."[1]

> *What did my fingers do before they held him?*
> *What did my heart do with its love?*
> *I have never seen a thing so dear.*
> *His lids are like the lilac-flower*
> *And soft as a moth, his breath.*
> *I shall not let go.*

If you have already had a baby, even ten years ago, you know all about this and can smile at the recollection; you think back to the feelings of utter incompetence, perhaps, the awful self-doubts, the panic, the emotional swings, the sweetness as the baby lay sleeping peacefully, the awesome responsibility of protecting and caring for this new life, the firmness of the rounded limbs against your body, the heaviness of the head as a feeding finishes in utter content, the fine down on the skin, and the scent of warm peaches.

A Whetted Appetite

Women having another baby after a long interval, although they may feel aghast at what they have done, and though at the beginning of pregnancy they may be resentful about being, as one woman said, "put back firmly in the home" and "trapped," look forward to these things with whetted appetite. They know it will be crazy and chaotic, but it is going to be fun! It is not just a question of the baby "keeping you young," either; it may feel once the baby is really there as if the choice is between rejuvenation and collapse.

The mother of a "surprise" baby often feels a special passionate closeness to the child. One said that this was "almost psychic." "Perhaps," she added, "we have to fight for their entry into this world that much more and the fight has provided the bond." She had faced the idea of abortion and after a struggle had decided firmly against it, in the face of other people's advice. One battle for this particular woman was against the horrified disapproval of her own mother, who would not speak to her for six months. Many women also feel that the hurdles of tests through which they go during pregnancy are also like part of a long struggle to have the baby.

When the older woman compares her experience with the late-born baby with how she was as a mother with earlier children, she always says how much more relaxed, confident, and at ease she is this time around. Motherhood is not just a matter of biology. A woman's attitude of mind is vital—the spirit in which she starts out on this new adventure. Women having a second family have a different time scale from even those older mothers who are having their first-born children, and say they spend time with the baby because everything else seems relatively unimportant. "I know that time passes all too quickly when children are small," remarks one mother, previously in educational research, "and that these early years are crucial for future learning, social behavior, and exploration." The experienced mother also realizes that problems that seem insurmountable at the time all pass before long. One who felt "cloistered" with her baby during feeding times that went on and on and on remembered that this stage was a temporary one, and reflected that she needed this time to get to know her baby properly and to protect herself from outside stresses.

For the first-time mother over thirty, the initial challenges appear rather different. Looking ahead to the enforced change of role, the excitement is mixed with anxiety, not just about coping, but about what the baby's arrival will do to her as a person. For a time it is delightful not to have to rush out and be "bright and interesting," but even while she basks in this satisfaction there may be stirrings of restlessness. This is intensified if the baby is at first unwanted. As one woman, commenting on the distress she experienced after the birth of her baby, said:

> I lost my personal space. My overriding preoccupation is how I am going to get back to work. At first I thought I'd probably have to give up work and felt very resentful of the baby. It was a tremendous upheaval to discover I was pregnant. I have a fantastic doctor and he made a lot of time to talk so that I didn't bottle this up inside. I decided, Yes, I do want to have the baby. Now I'm anxious about how we are going to get along. Will we like each other? How are we going to sort this one out together?

Her opportunity to talk freely with her doctor helped her move beyond concern solely with what the birth of the baby was going to do to *her* to concern with her relationship with this new person. Without the opportunity to talk, that progression might have been delayed until well after the baby came.

A Career Crisis

For a career woman, having a baby provokes a crisis that she often realizes may never be resolved. One new mother, completely committed to her career and unwilling to take time out from it, said her mind was only set at rest when her obstetrician said, "Right! I promise to keep you working as long as I can and to get you back to work as soon as possible afterward." Many women are far less sure that this is what they want. They do not know whether they will want to go back to work, or if they intend to do so, how soon they and the baby will be ready for this. Shall it be job, baby, or job and baby? Within the European Community, it is now the law that a woman cannot be dismissed from her job because of pregnancy.

The decision as to whether, in fact, you want to return is yours, and you can change your mind at any time. If you say when you leave that you do not want to return, however, you are closing the door on the options open to you. But 46 percent of women are not eligible for maternity rights and fewer than 1 percent of those working eight to sixteen hours a week qualify. For if you work only part-time before you take maternity leave, or have not been in the same employment for a period of two years, these regulations do not apply.

In the United States, maternity- and family-leave policies are much less favorable to new mothers. Six weeks of unpaid leave and assurance of keeping her job is the best policy most American women can look forward to. Some use up paid sick leave and vacation time in order to spend more time at home with their new babies.

A pregnant woman may be very uncertain of what her feelings are going to be after the baby arrives and perhaps does not trust that she is ever going to fall in love with her baby.

"Your career is about to take off or is already well established," Tricia explained. "For me it was the problem of when to break and that if I did have two or three years out it would be difficult to get back in."

Virginia said she planned to earn a postgraduate degree to "keep her mind awake" and was afraid that having a baby would muddle her brain unless she took determined steps to develop new career skills.

Financial problems may loom large, not because of an overall shortage of money but because a woman in her thirties is usually earning more than she did ten years before and the disappearance of one partner's salary makes a dramatic difference. She is often anxious about the loss of independence and freedom that come from having her own income:

Thinking of being financially dependent on my husband upsets me. I've been independent for so long. I feel trapped by the thought that I have to ask for money for the everyday things of life, having to say, "Please, can I have twenty dollars because I can't get through this month?" or "Would you mind paying the electric bill?"

A woman who says she is "lucky" because she works two hours a day at home designing children's clothes says that without this and her own money she might feel frustrated. The dependence that is being fought against is more than economic. For many women it expresses anxiety about a loss of selfhood.

The fear is that you are somehow going to be sucked in by baby care, your brain will turn into a vegetable, and you will become "just a mother." A woman to whom children are stuck like "barnacles encrusting a ship and limpets clinging to a rock" is the awful image summoned up by Margaret Atwood in *The Edible Woman*.[2] For the committed feminist there is the inherent threat that she has "sold out" to motherhood and to a role stereotype that legitimizes the social inferiority of women. One woman said that her feminist friends "are upset at my loss of independence, and opting out."

First-time mothers look very carefully at their friends and relations who have small children. They watch them with all the vigilance and concentration of an ethologist observing a pack of orangutans. And they tend to come away highly critical of what they see.

Total Devotion?

A group of pregnant women having first babies in their thirties were discussing the kind of mother they hoped to be. They were all anxious about devoting themselves entirely to a baby.

"I know a couple who haven't been out to dinner with each other for eighteen months," Maureen said.

"It's the same with friends of ours," said another. "But she's a very awkward baby. She won't sleep for longer than three hours and she is just so tired."

"I get rather cross at the relish with which other women say, 'Oh, you won't have a minute to yourself, you won't have time to read a book,'" Julia protested. "They seem to *enjoy* saying this. I just cannot imagine not having time to read or to write a letter. I can't imagine being so tired. It makes me very depressed."

"From some of the things people say," Jan exclaimed, "I get the feeling that I'm expected to metamorphize into a completely different person. Two friends who are doctors and who were at the peaks of their careers said, 'It's wonderful to vegetate at home.' I don't think it will be. I have a fear that something *biological* will happen to me."

Another woman remarked that even during her pregnancy friends seem to be distancing themselves. "It's almost as if being pregnant is supposed to affect your decision making and therefore your opinions are not worth listening to (though your partner's are)."

The contrast between these anxieties and the surge of emotion that comes with being a new mother is startling. The woman no longer seems to be protecting herself in the same way. Joan, a nurse for twenty years who had her first baby at thirty-eight, said she feared that she had thrown away her last vestige of independence forever when she became pregnant. She went on from there to describe the emotional journey into motherhood.

After a difficult and painful seventeen-hour labor, she had a forceps delivery and her baby was taken immediately to the intensive-care nursery.

I confess I was relieved not to have to take care of him the first night as I was deeply shocked by all the pain. But during the days that followed I was filled with pure delight at this little person who I found hard to believe was really mine. I appreciate that having babies is old hat to most people and there is nothing unique about my experience, but the feelings that came to me

so unexpectedly were ones of overwhelming emotion for which I
felt I had been ill-prepared. Sometimes I was torn apart by the
thought that something might happen to the baby. He means
much more to me than I had imagined.

Bonding

In the mid-1970s two pediatricians became fascinated by the emotional intensity of which they became aware as they observed mothers with their newborn babies and analyzed what went on between
them.[3] Doctors had discovered mother love. They started to learn
about the dialogue that begins within seconds of birth when a
woman is able to hold her newborn baby and to gaze into her
child's eyes. A system that attempts to facilitate this process has
now been incorporated into care in many hospitals in the West. It
is called "bonding." Caregivers are supposed to allow time for it,
to check that it is occurring, and in some hospitals to record this
in the patient's chart.

The medical takeover of mother love involves the use of ultrasound in the pregnancy, too. Observing that mothers are surprised,
delighted, and intrigued when they "see" their babies on the ultrasound screen, some obstetricians assert that this should be included as a routine part of care to enable mothers to fall in love
with their babies. The thinking here is that love is too important
to be left to mothers. It must be integrated into obstetric management.[4] Yet mothers have eagerly reached out their arms for their
babies and have fallen passionately in love with them for thousands
of years before doctors sought to take control of this emotional
transformation. Indeed, if it becomes—like dilatation of the cervix
and the length of the first and second stages of labor—a process
that is medically managed, there is a real risk that doctors may do
more harm than good.

The emotions that flood in as the baby is lifted out of your body
are often unexpected and seem to have no connection with more
conventional ideas of love. Some older women who have had no

experience of small babies and have read about the importance of bonding are anxious that they will not be able to respond with appropriate emotions, and that those present will criticize them for their inability to bond. In fact, for any mother there is often a phase of stunned astonishment, an interval when she needs time to find herself again. Moira expressed this when she said:

> The head oozed out and then the shoulders were eased through. He came out resembling a little lizard. All my emotions were frozen in a void with this beautiful yet very ugly creature lying on my tummy. Then Tony [her husband] told us how terrific we were, which made the moment very special.

The first-time mother, whatever her age, is often rather frightened of her child at first. "I thought she was lovely," one woman said, "but was scared and lived in a fog of worry and uncertainty until she was six weeks old. Then the fog cleared miraculously and there we were, the three of us intact."

The change that takes place is partly biological. The woman at term is primed physiologically and psychologically for motherhood. The release of hormones into her bloodstream during and following labor (the rush of oxytocin which is still incompletely understood) is linked with uterine contractions, working to open the cervix and press the baby down the birth canal. The same hormonal surge subsequently contracts the uterus to expel the placenta and mold it back into its former shape, and drive her forward emotionally into motherhood, too. She is carried on a wave of powerful emotions, a passion that is for many women intensely sexual in its pain and pleasure. Michel Odent describes oxytocin as "the happiness hormone," released only when the woman feels she can trust herself and her body. This and other hormones flood her bloodstream during the days following birth, making her emotionally labile, vulnerable, but above all, responsible.

This acute physiological link with the baby lasts for many women for about six weeks, and for some much longer. It corresponds to the period of "primary maternal preoccupation" described by Donald Winnicott, the pediatrician and psychotherapist, although the term does nothing to convey the powerful "gut feelings" and the almost animal nature of the bond between the mother and her newborn. It has clearly been important to the survival of the species.

Giving—and Receiving

The new mother is often enormously surprised to discover her capacity for selfless giving and patience far beyond her expectations. She is in partnership with her baby, sending out signals involving touch, scent, the rhythm of her breathing and heartbeats; her eyes are turned toward the baby and her voice raised to a higher than usual pitch, as she speaks in a pattern of five- to fifteen-second intervals and quite unconsciously repeats the phrases with a strong beat that have meaning for all babies and in all languages.

Apparently casual, random behavior is, in fact, perfectly adjusted to the needs and attention span of this new baby. The mother leans forward so that she is face-to-face with her baby and about a forearm's length away, the distance at which the child can most easily focus on her shining eyes and mobile mouth, and the one at which a baby is naturally held when breast-feeding. She raises her eyebrows quite spontaneously and begins to talk. The baby's attention is caught by the movement. She smiles and the relief planes of her face are increased. In a questioning tone of voice, reiterating simple syllables, she starts to "rev up" the baby, exaggerating her facial expression, perhaps grimacing, and she may do that over and over again, like an angler throwing a line. At last the baby catches on and gets excited. Eyes light up; the lips form a shape; there may be a little gurgle or coo of pleasure. The relationship between mother and baby is a going concern!

Far from being a passive little bundle, the newborn baby seeks stimulation, explores, and starts out on a new adventure. The child, too, is sending out signals and plays an active role in this partnership. She gazes at her mother's forehead and she hovers nearer, trying to catch her eyes. Then she gets her attention, and in the early days for a brief time only, the two begin a conversation together, until the baby gets bored with it and her attention wanders. The anxious mother continues to hover and try to stimulate the baby to respond. The relaxed one releases the baby to turn to something else of interest, or to be fairly passive until the next burst of conversation between them. It is as if the two are learning a dance together. When the mother is anxious or depressed, or the baby is suffering the effects of pain-relieving drugs received from her bloodstream during labor, or has a headache from a difficult birth, it takes longer for them to learn that dance of interaction. But it is astonishing how many mothers and babies, even though the mother feels she has no "maternal instincts" or has worried that she will be "tied down" by a baby or that her "mind will rot," start to enjoy each other.

They both have the advantage of much more primitive nonverbal signals, too, than we are inclined to acknowledge in adult life. Smell is one of them. Many new mothers comment on the delicious scent of their babies. The baby, for her part, responds to the mother's smell. Dr. Aidan MacFarlane, an Oxford pediatrician, has shown that even five-day-old babies prefer a breast pad that has been against their own mother's breast to one worn by a strange mother. The maternal scent is intensified by heat produced in the mother's breasts as she responds to her baby's cry. It is not only the smell of milk but a scent emanating from her skin that the baby senses. This is partly because the woman who has recently delivered is very warm and during the first days after birth perspires freely, losing the fluid that was retained in her tissues in the last weeks of pregnancy. I do not know of anything that has ever been written about the smell of puerperal blood. We usually treat it as merely a messy waste-product, an aftermath of childbirth. But it has a strong, clinging, and exciting smell that is in some ways intensely sexual. The baby cannot fail to be aware of this afterbirth blood scent. As the baby sucks at the breast, oxytocin makes the uterus contract further and more blood is squeezed out, sometimes (especially early in the morning, after lying down for some hours) in heavy velvety clots.

For a woman who has not yet had her baby this may seem revolting. But with birth come strange new pleasures, deep below the level of our conscious being and having nothing to do with the more conventional pleasures of having a baby. It is as well to have a mind open to them, too.

Eager to Learn

At the same time a good deal of more obvious cerebral activity is taking place. If you watch carefully, you can see that the baby is eager and quick to learn. Wait until she is in a quiet, alert state, comfortable with her body, not hungry, but wide awake and staring at you. Then stick out your tongue. The chances are that after a few false starts there will be a flicker of movement from the baby's mouth and she, too, will try to put out her tongue. After a few days

Then stick out your tongue . . .

of this game, done only when the baby is happy and attentive, she will mimic you effectively. It is the beginning of a great game. It is on such copying that the learning of language and the more general acquisition of culture is based in each society. Long before speech, the patterns of mouth movements and even facial expressions are already set.

It is important to let the baby set the pace. The overstimulated baby, entertained too vigorously by an adult who wants to prove that he or she can be successful, turns away and gazes hard at something else, ignoring the brash stimulus and making the intruder feel rejected. If this happens too often, a parent can feel like a failure. Some babies enjoy more stimuli than others. You need to get to know your baby. If you act just according to the book, or set an educational scheme going that is insensitive to what your baby is telling you, the relationship is hampered from the start.

While the trigger for all this is a biological one, important in creating the bonds of the family and the handing on of culture in all human communities, the specific scene is that offered by the environment in which the mother first meets and begins to get to know her baby. For most women in the Western world nowadays, this is a hospital. The atmosphere provided in that setting can help or inhibit bonding. This atmosphere is only indirectly created by curtains or furnishings. It is made by *people*.

The way the relationship starts is not entirely dependent on what is happening during the time following delivery. It is in part an outcome of everything that has happened to the mother in labor and while she was pregnant. She has not been merely a container for the fetus. What she feels about the act of birth and the care she is given, the way she is treated as a person, not just as a caretaker for the baby, affects her ability to relate to her child. When she feels cherished and among friends, free to act spontaneously without stopping to wonder whether she is doing the right thing or obeying the rules or reaching a set standard, she can most enjoy her baby.

With loving emotional support and in a relaxed atmosphere, the

The overstimulated baby

most unlikely woman starts out on motherhood with gusto. It is not a matter of doing the "right" thing; there is no right way to take care of a baby. It is more a matter of doing what you feel like doing and not getting self-conscious about it. Even if you do not get the chance to be yourself while you are still in the hospital, and do not fall in love with your baby until after you come home, you need not feel that you have missed a limited opportunity that time and circumstances have gobbled up. In human relationships there are always, fortunately, second, third, and even fourth chances. Each of the anxious pregnant women who were discussing their fears about the future and their loss of self-esteem discovered that they were surprised at the pleasure they found in what one called "the exquisite beauty of captivity to a baby."

A Support Network

If you are expecting your first baby after thirty-five, it is a good idea to contact other women in the same age group who are having or have just had their babies. Your doctor or midwife may be able to help. Your prenatal teacher or the local childbirth education association certainly can. It is not only useful to get together beforehand to discuss the changes in your lives. It may also be helpful to have a support network afterward, and to know that there is someone you can call who is tackling similar difficulties. Many childbirth education organizations have postnatal support groups. You can either use the existing structure or get something going yourself that is specifically for older first-time mothers. One woman said, "I got depressed. The baby was demanding and cried a lot, and I felt I'd put myself back sixteen years to when I had my first baby in my teens. Then I found a drop-in play group, and I felt part of a community of women. I hooked up with the postnatal network, too. They are coffee mornings, yes, but quite different from other coffee mornings. They're fantastically valuable."

It can take some courage to make new contacts after the baby comes, and it may be difficult to get out to meet other people unless you have arranged things in advance. A new mother of forty, whose friends all had children in their teens, said it was a totally alien world to her, and it was not until she started taking her child to a play group that she caught up with social contacts that otherwise would have passed her by.

I meet these efficient twenty- to twenty-five-year-olds wisely discussing child management and nursery groups. For all my gray hairs I think it must be good to have this link with a much younger group. Perhaps it will keep me feeling younger, if I'm not worn out by the effort.

Ellen went through a difficult time when her little daughter was three to six months old, a time when the novelty of having a baby has worn off and when most women find endlessly repeated tasks are beginning to get them down. With Ellen it was particularly hard because Penny was awake most of the day, sleeping only four half-hour stretches:

> Unlike what the books say she was definitely *not* happy sitting in her bouncing chair and watching Mommy doing things. *She* wanted to be doing things and found it very frustrating that she couldn't. She therefore wanted my constant attention so we could "do" things together.

Ellen felt she was "foundering in a sea of baby and wondering if I'd ever surface." She started shouting at her baby, and was then submerged in guilt. Her husband could not help, as he had just started making a new film and came home late each evening, emotionally and physically drained. She began to feel very lonely and to long for adult company:

> I met a mother who was part of the local clinic. She was part of the local postnatal support group. From then on I never looked back. I became involved with other mothers with similar interests and background (in their thirties, had careers, etc.). I had people to share my new experiences and difficulties with, and we gave each other support.

She started helping other mothers who were still at a stage through which she had passed and says this gave her "a tremendous feeling of being of use to others apart from my baby." Through working with this postnatal support group, Ellen weaned herself from the state of total immersion in her baby. It is this period that can be so long and drawn-out and painful for the socially isolated mother.

Feeling Tired

Your only chance of catching up on sleep may be to allow yourself to drift off when the baby sleeps during the day (all babies sleep *sometimes*). It is difficult to do this when people expect you to be up and about, the phone is ringing, and there is noise outside. But a late-morning or early-afternoon siesta can refresh and rejuvenate. Some people can drop off to sleep for ten minutes and wake up refreshed. But for many this is worse than not going to sleep at all. A normal sleep cycle lasts ninety minutes, so this is the ideal length for a siesta, if you can get it. But the quality as well as the length of sleep is important. To sink into a deep sleep, it helps to be in a darkened room, perhaps with music as a screen against other intrusive sound. Although it may take superhuman efforts to make this space in your life, it may be the only weapon that an older mother can seize against the fatigue that many experience, especially in the early days.

Some women need more than this—complete seclusion with the baby, taking naps whenever the baby lets them, and—for a time, at any rate—a screening out of the external world. As a woman gets to know her baby, discovers his rhythms, and develops self-confidence, the extreme tiredness begins to slip away.

One woman said that both she and her husband were "terrified":

Having had no contact with infants, we relied on books. I put myself into voluntary purdah, determined not to surface until I had established my confidence.

This experience was rewarding because she found the relationship with her partner strengthened by it. "Sharing care of Jenny has been the longest sole period of shared activity in our thirteen years." On the other hand, many of those mothers who write within two years of a child's birth say that libido is much reduced, they are too exhausted for sex, and make love much less frequently than before conception.

One woman, whose youngest child is now five, says, "The baby was so demanding and I was so tired I am surprised that the marriage survived at all sometimes." She says she had "nothing left over" for her husband, "nothing left to give." The first eighteen months were "a dark, black patch" in her life.

Once this period is over, most couples seem to rediscover their sex lives if they have not grown apart with diametrically opposed social roles and responsibilities, in the meantime.

The loss of personal time—time in which *you* can decide what you want to do, or simply to do nothing—comes as a shock. A thirty-eight-year-old woman with a twenty-month-old and a new baby says, "My personal time is now my time with the baby, when Matt takes the older one out. I miss freewheeling brain time. There is the constant tension of having to plan ahead. I look at my friends with babies and realize that men rarely plan ahead. Women have to do it—checking the contents of the changing bag when you go out, deciding the time when you *can* go out—always looking ahead."

At forty-five, with children of twenty, eighteen, fourteen, and ten weeks, Diana is enjoying the changed form of the family, which now spreads across three generations (since her mother is alive); she says that the birth has "thrilled and rejuvenated" her. Diana claims that

> The adventure of producing and supporting this new personality is more interesting than the alternatives of middle-age career, more holidays, and outings. Our new arrival has come at an age when many of our friends are tired, bored, frustrated, and wondering what to do with themselves!

The experience has made life richer for this couple, and they feel much younger.

It is obvious that it is not just a question of learning new and difficult technical tasks. For the woman who has been engaged in work that has a beginning, middle, and end, caring for a baby poses an entirely new activity of a kind that is never finished and that she can never assess completely. As one woman put it:

> I find it difficult with young children to work at full stretch with my attention divided in several different directions at once. Having been exhorted at school to "keep your eye on the ball" and "concentrate on the job at hand," I was not prepared for this.

Another, listing the things she has learned since she had her baby, says they are (1) rarely finishing a conversation; (2) never eating a meal leisurely; (3) drinking cold tea and coffee; and (4) getting jobs done while the baby is asleep. All this makes her feel that external events are "manipulating" her. This is sometimes made more acute for the woman who has had her first baby in her late thirties because of what one calls "a heightened awareness of problems and perhaps taking the whole experience more seriously, as a commitment and responsibility." It is this, rather than simply a failure in resilience or lack of physical energy, that proves most tiring. Many women say they go on in faith, not really knowing whether they are doing well or badly. There are a million and one tasks, repetitive and mundane, none of which are rewarded and most of which go unnoticed by anybody, but these are only incidental to the main activity, which is completely amorphous and which continues day and night. To have to face this alone and without the support of a loving partner can be a nightmare.

Yet having a partner and other family members involved does not necessarily make it any simpler. For although it is possible to draw sustenance from their concern and caring, the birth means that radical changes have to be worked through together and new understanding sought, and this can be a painful process. Tiredness and confusion may mean that communication breaks down, and that the person who is most trying to help proves to be the most irritating. The birth of a child in an already formed family, or to a couple who have been together for some time and have formed a modus vivendi for just the two of them, compels adjustment in a whole network of relationships. People caught up in this begin to see themselves and each other in a new light. It can be a major growth experience in middle age.

7

Partners

Babies thrive when they are cared for by more than one loving adult. This simple fact, reflecting the kind of cherishing in the family that babies receive all over the world, has been obscured by psychological pronouncements on the part of experts who have threatened mothers with causing incalculable damage to their infants if they did not commit themselves to full-time mothering, day in and day out, for the first three years of the child's life.

The power of John Bowlby's work to grip women with fear that they were neglecting and depriving their children when they handed them over to another adult for a well-earned break affected a whole generation of mothers and often made them feel resentful of the baby who was trapping them within four walls, and guilty that they felt the resentment.[1] It was not, of course, Dr. Bowlby's fault. His research was caught up in an insidious social force that in the 1950s was driving women back to their homes to be good wives and mothers and telling them that they ought to find all their fulfillment there. If you could not, you were not a "real" woman. Mothers reared children, collected thread spools and empty cartons to make educational playthings, baked bread, and cultivated the domestic arts as if their lives depended on it. We thought we were doing the best for our children. Some struggled to do things outside the home as well, but without our husbands or children noticing.

Your mother's and your partner's mother's standards of child rearing may have been very much influenced by this. You may feel under some pressure to show them that you can cope and be just as good a mother as they were. Or you may feel that you can never reach their standard and will always be a failure in their eyes. Or you may be impatient with their mothering style and want to demonstrate that you are doing things quite differently, and even imply that they were fools to make all the sacrifices that were necessary to follow the advice of these psychology experts. To be understood, mothering always has to be seen in its historical and social context; and once we understand the pressures on women, and the ways in which mothers are forced to fit into a ready-made mold, we can begin to understand ourselves and our own mothers better.

It is easy for a mother to make herself essential to a small child, easy to build such an intense one-to-one relationship, with no room for any other adult's participation, that the child cannot be left with anyone else, will not accept comfort from them, and suffers an acute trauma of separation if the mother attempts to cut the bond. The woman whose only emotional rewards are in her family may make herself indispensable to her children because otherwise she is nothing.

In societies in which other family members and friends and neighbors share in the care of small children, the child moves easily from one to the other. Of course she knows who her mother is, even if the compound is shared with her co-wives and their children, but the relationship is not so exclusive that it rules out other attachments. The mother-child tie is one of a whole pattern of rich relationships. Among the Ganda, researchers Schaffer and Emerson found that by the time babies were eighteen months old, all but a handful of children were emotionally attached to more than one person, and often to several.[2] The father was most likely to be the chief of these attachment figures. But toddlers were also attached to older children who acted as caregivers.

Women ought to find their fulfillment in the home . . .

There is a very special time in the life of any mother and baby when the relationship is intense in a different way, which I touched on earlier. This is during the first six to eight weeks of the child's life, the period that Donald Winnicott called "primary maternal preoccupation," when the psychophysiological bond of a lactating mother to her infant is often so strong that it preempts other relationships, seems to blot out the rest of the world, and causes her to respond to and protect her baby like a tigress defending her young. "I had never realized before," one woman said, "how much I was an animal—gloriously so." Some women say that this affects all their emotions, which become more concentrated and more passionately experienced.

A Primitive Bond

This phase of new motherhood is so distinct that anybody else behaving in such a way would be considered pathologically disturbed. Yet it is a natural part of being a mother. It is the recognition of this primitive bond between mother and neonate that has in some ways been allowed to spill over into the whole of the rest of motherhood, and is sometimes accepted as the norm for women with ten-month-old babies, and two-year-old and four-year-old and eight-year-old children. When the mother cannot function in this emotional intensity or feels crushed by the demands made on her, she believes there must be something wrong with her.

The woman starting out on motherhood in her thirties or forties for the first time is often rather afraid of this. She has watched other women with babies and from the vantage point of her career has seen what has happened to fellow students and colleagues. This may be one reason why she has put off having a child. She wanted freedom to live her own life first, to put her education to some use, to achieve something. As one put it, "I needed to protect my individuality." Another said, "I feel I was conditioned by what everyone else wanted to do or has done. I needed to free myself to think out what I wanted to do and make it my own decision." And yet another:

> I was an independent, ambitious career woman with a happy marriage based on the principle of equality. I regard this stage of motherhood [with little ones] as temporary and a temporary pause in my career development. I imagine I will return to my former dynamic, individual, ambitious self. If I had had a baby in my twenties I would have found motherhood claustrophobic, crippling my independence and freedom. I couldn't even consider marriage then, so strong was my desire to be free.

She is sometimes aware that in a way she "mothers" her partner and is anxious lest the baby's claims for attention compete with his. It is important for them to discuss such anxieties in advance of the birth. A good childbirth class in which there is plenty of free discussion and sharing among expectant parents lets them do just that and discover that other couples have the same doubts and apprehensions. Penny and Leo have been together five years. His mother left him as a baby and he was brought up by his father. Penny said she knew she mothered him: "That side is strong in our relationship. Sometimes he says, 'I won't be your baby anymore.' He feels threatened by the baby. But I have seen him with small babies and he's lovely with them. I've tried to reassure him."

Prue comments on what Penny is saying: "I feel the same with my husband. It was my decision to have the baby and there was no encouragement. But I've seen him with children. He's changed a lot with the pregnancy. First of all he wasn't interested at all. He was worried and said, 'I don't feel old enough to have a family.' He didn't want to be tied down. Now he's looking forward to it— he's totally changed."

Lyn says:

When I first realized I was pregnant, Dick's attitude was, "Oh God!" He used to treat children like Martians, incomprehensible! He stood back from them. Now I've noticed him seeming more relaxed, not just with children, but a kind of emotional freedom. He used to be very self-contained emotionally. The pregnancy has given a legitimate channel for feelings which have been kept out and which he has never expressed before. This has had a very positive effect on our relationship.

The dynamics of psychological change when a couple share together the emotional as well as the physical preparation for a baby are such that each is better able to meet the stresses that come afterward and enjoy the inevitable change in their relationship. As one woman said, it was not only that they were very happy about the pregnancy, it was also a "bonding" of two people.

Shared Responsibility

A loving partner who shares parenting with an equal sense of responsibility is the foundation of life for those women who describe themselves as happy and confident mothers. One woman looking back eighteen years later to the birth of her twins at thirty-five and the subsequent experience of parenting with a husband who, she says, "took a full share in caring for the children from the start" comments:

> We have discovered ourselves. There is a whole area of one's character that emerges in parenthood, in the way one copes . . . and in communicating with one's children. This has been a continuing surprise over the years.

This partner is often a husband, sometimes a lover, sometimes another woman, but the woman alone without anyone to share parenting, or who struggles to bring up a child while her partner is immersed in career and success outside the home, is invariably at a disadvantage. The majority of women who wrote made explicit statements about ways in which they worked out together their joint commitment as parents. A woman having her first baby at this age who has worked outside the home over a period of some years, together sharing household chores in an egalitarian way, is more likely to plan a strategy of this kind with her partner than women who already have families and who go on to have another baby or start another family after an interval, sometimes with a new husband. It is the middle-aged second husband who tends to see his main responsibilities as outside the home and to leave child care exclusively to his wife.

But for any man who feels under pressure at work and is climbing a career ladder, home tends to be "off-duty" time when peace and quiet, contentment and some conviviality are expected. He feels under heavy financial responsibility and looks on home as a place of relaxation where he can enjoy an interval with his wife and child. These are the fathers who play with their children and sometimes "help" but who feel no responsibility for child care. Some of these women who are left "holding the baby" sound a note of regret and some obviously feel trapped in their roles as mothers, at least for the time being, and are critical of the absent partner.

Olivia had one child at twenty-seven and her second at thirty-six, after having been told by her gynecologist that she would not be able to have any more children and failing to adopt. Laurence is a university lecturer. Olivia says that he helped much more with the first baby, because

> he was very jealous of my ability to feed him and wanted to do everything for him that he could. This time Laurence isn't at home as much. His job is very demanding and time-consuming and he travels away from home frequently. He has perhaps changed the baby's diaper a dozen times in seventeen months and gets up with her in the morning once a week if I'm lucky. Our roles have become more "typed" than ten years ago. Laurence's work has very high priority for all of us. We don't have the equality of job prospects that we shared in our early twenties.

Una is forty, with children aged thirteen, eleven, and nine, and before the birth of her new baby was a part-time college lecturer. Her husband has long days in the office and gets home late, so does not help with the domestic work or the children. Una says, "I wonder whether I'll ever be able to get a job now, with my age and the numbers of unemployed increasing together. I have pangs of jealousy at my husband's career success, as I was just as brainy and well qualified as he was once. What really bugs me is that if he wants a regular evening out he can have one. If *I* want a regular evening out, he says I can have one, but then has to be away with his job." She confesses that she feels intellectually frustrated and resentful.

Teresa has just had her second baby after postpartum depression for a year following her first child's birth. Her firstborn is now two and a quarter, and it is clear from the way she writes that puerperal hormone changes give a very inadequate explanation for the de-

Laurence is a university lecturer . . .

pression into which she is sinking again. Her husband was "thrilled" with the pregnancy but, she says,

> I'd have appreciated help with shopping and heavy housework.
> I deeply resented him for not offering, after I'd said a couple of
> times I needed help, and I was too proud to go on asking. He
> thinks of fatherhood as having a "nice cuddle" and playing with
> "pretty, well-cared-for kids," but should also have the experience
> of disposing of the daily piles of grubby clothes and dirty diapers,
> planning and cooking balanced meals, and shopping for them
> and tidying up toys. He's very good at entertaining David for
> hours but leaves a stream of toys, books, used cups, and clothes
> in his wake, which are apparently invisible to him once they
> have served their purpose. If I go out it doesn't occur to him to
> plan and produce a meal for the child.

She worked full-time till David was nine months old, a very
stressful period because she felt torn between the child and her
work and felt that total responsibility for him and the running of
the home fell on her. "When David was ill it was always me who
took time off from work. Men have a long way to go," she con-

cludes, "before they are truly fathers the way women are mothers to their children."

Conditioned Mothers

It is not just that men often take it for granted that women are responsible for baby care and domestic work and expect them to be better at looking after babies than they are; it is also that women themselves are socially conditioned to feel *they* ought to be home-makers and child rearers to such an extent that they may shut the father out of full participation in parenting. Jill, age thirty-six and doing part-time teaching, cannot help herself, the emotions are so strong. She feels depressed, tired, and "in a state of confusion about my roles of mother/wife/worker," and weighed down by "a terrible responsibility." Yet "even though I trust my husband when he is dealing with Sean, I feel that *I* am on duty. I hover and remind him of things. He would rather be left to get on with it! Our relationship as a couple has been very much affected. I have become aware that at times I exclude Mike in my baby-centered world . . . we are like ships passing in a fog."

The marriages of some of the mothers who wrote had already broken up under this kind of strain. Hannah, for instance, says that the relationship "foundered under the stress of responsibilities which I was left to bear." They now live on different levels of a big house. She brings up her son, but his father is "his best play partner and brings him many things which I cannot offer."

The social isolation that many mothers feel with their small children is peculiar to our Western, urban society. In Muslim societies, which represent for many in the West the epitome of female subjugation, women have a vigorous and highly colorful autonomous world in their own quarters, from which men are excluded.[3] A sisterhood of women share in child care, both in the practical tasks and the emotional support of the new mother.

The Indian woman is similarly part of a group consisting of her husband's brothers' wives, his mother, and his unmarried sisters.

There is no privacy, but at the same time there is no loneliness.[4]

In the Caribbean, women are part of a sisterhood network, helping, gossiping about, counseling, and sharing with one another, bemoaning their lot at the hands of men who are good for nothing, and striving in common to feed their children, clothe them, get them through school, and "grow them right." In each village, three leaders, all women, act as primary communicators between every household: the postmistress, the schoolmistress, and the midwife.[5] In rural areas, to be isolated is impossible, and the same pattern of social organization infiltrates the life of the clusters of shack dwellings and the homes of the poor in the towns.

Women are often told that depression suffered after childbirth is the result of major hormonal changes, and the distress they feel is all attributed to physiological processes over which they have no control. Although this may be cheering for some, for at least it is not their "fault," it perpetuates the misery for many women, who are thereby absolved from the responsibility or opportunity to change the social conditions in which they function from day to day as mothers, which are the real cause of their distress. It is only too easy for a man, also, to explain a woman's depression by reference to her hormones and, apart from urging her to see the doctor, do nothing else about it. If she does go to the doctor, drug treatment often does not cure her. A controlled test of the commonly prescribed antidepressant imipramine revealed that it was no better than a placebo.[6]

To be alone in a house with total responsibility for a screaming baby who seems to be crying *at* you and telling you what a hopeless mother you are is a *social* situation which has nothing to do with whether you have a uterus and breasts. One woman said, "I go and hide in the bathroom when she cries. Maybe I do that instead of throwing her down the stairs." It is not only mothers who do this. Distraught baby-sitters who cannot quiet an infant do it, too.

Physicians, public health nurses, health visitors, childbirth educators, and other counselors continue to reassure the new mother that all that is needed is a readjustment of hormones, an attitude that stems from a uterine psychology that had its origins in the

Middle Ages and from concepts of hysteria as the result of a wandering womb. Freudian theory reinforced this ideology of the female mind as a direct consequence of anatomy and laid down that a woman's reproductive system was "the site for the acting out of impulses, especially aggression, and its derivative, sex anxiety, and maternity-pregnancy fears."[7] No such claims have been made about men's mood swings, the inference being that they are more purely cerebral and less chained to their physiology. Yet, as Ann Oakley points out,[8] monthly cycles have been reported for men in body temperature,[9] weight,[10] and beard growth,[11] and pain threshold and cyclical rhythms have been discovered in emotional changes,[12] urine levels of hormones,[13] and schizophrenia, manic depression, and epilepsy.[14]

The Father's Role

In fact it cannot be assumed that women are the only ones to experience postpartum depression. Childbirth is a major life crisis for many couples, and becoming a father can be just as stressful for a man as the transition to motherhood is for a woman. Sometimes a man is so overwhelmed by his own feelings that he is unable to give the woman the emotional support she needs. As men get more involved in the experience of birth, not just as watchers or members of a supporting cast, but as full emotional participants, they encounter many of the psychological conflicts that are typical of the passage to new social roles. They, too, experience the primary preoccupation with the baby, which until now has been thought to be a female characteristic.

If it is believed that men must always be strong, that they must not show their emotions, and that their main task is to provide economic support, leaving all the feeling to the woman, this may be seen as an unfortunate social development. But this emotional involvement means that couples have a chance to share in being parents and be open with each other as never before. Those who experience it find it an enriching and often completely unexpected bonus of parenthood.

It can be hard for a man to get involved with a baby and bond when she has been produced by the hospital as a specialist medical product and he feels that the whole process of having a baby is so risky that it is best to leave it all to the "experts." Fathers, like mothers, also find it difficult to develop confidence in handling the baby if they feel they are second-rate caregivers and that someone is watching to see that they do it properly. There are some situations in which both parents are more likely to feel that the baby is the property of the hospital and to be very apprehensive about taking on responsibility for this precious new life. When a baby has been in intensive care, especially in a hospital where parent participation is not encouraged, a man may feel so anxious that the simplest solution seems to him to be to get out of the house and concentrate on his work.

In those intensive-care nurseries, however, where both parents are welcome at any time of the day or night and are shown how they can help take care of their baby, confidence develops very early. Most of the studies that have been published about this emphasize the benefits for the mother.[15] But the effect on the father is often astonishing, and changes an understandable hesitation and fear in handling his baby to supercompetence and pleasure in a matter of a few hours. The self-confidence he develops then indirectly can help the mother, too, and gives her the emotional support she needs. It sometimes seems that the emotional energy that is released when a man tends to his very tiny or sick baby flows beyond the infant and in a mysterious way enables the mother to feel cherished, too. Perhaps not having to go on as if nothing had happened and keep a stiff upper lip allows him to come closer to her feelings so that they share this difficult emotional journey with more understanding of each other's vulnerability.

Although Michael's first view of his eight-week premature twins in intensive care was, he says, "very fearsome" because they were wired up to "things going bleep, bleep, bop," he says that when he visited the unit after that first time he hardly noticed the apparatus, only his babies. He had to overcome apprehension about interfering with the smooth running of the unit but quickly realized that the staff were welcoming and wanted him there: "We were all in it together."

One of the babies was suffering from RDS, respiratory distress syndrome, because her lungs were inadequately inflated. Their normal lining, like the bubbles in detergent, was only partially present, and as a result her lungs collapsed between each breath and the sides stuck together like plastic bags. Then she had to make a terrific gasping effort to take the next breath.

Michael stood over her in the plastic box in which she struggled for life, feeling helpless to do anything, until a nurse suggested that he should hold her hand. As he did so he felt not only compassion and love, but as if the baby were giving *him* comfort. He started to stroke the little arm and talk to her soothingly. "She seemed to relax," he said. The baby was linked to an apparatus that measured the amount of oxygen in her blood. He had been shown how to read this, and to his surprise he saw that when he stimulated her in this way the oxygen content went up from about sixty to ninety. After three-quarters of an hour doing this, he noticed that she liked the inside of her thigh stroked and seemed to "feel safer." She began to breathe more easily, and he again saw the results on the oxygen meter.

Michael's relationship with his baby is a far cry from that of another father, who, though, his wife Janet says, is "close" to his son, needed her encouragement to "become involved on the physical side, changing diapers, bathing him, feeding him, etc. As with most domestic matters," she explains, "he'd rather not be involved so, and finds it easier now the child is two and a half, can communicate, and is not just an object with needs." This baby was born six weeks early by cesarean section and spent time in an intensive-care unit that was less liberal and welcoming to parents. He developed jaundice and was taken back there again. Though she does not say how her partner feels, Janet says she felt "intimidated" while in the hospital.

Breaking Down Barriers

A father's relationship with his new baby affects his relationship with his partner, too. It may have been partly because Michael was so stirred by the experience with his little daughter that he could be honest about his emotions. She said, "I can have a good cry without him thinking I'm stupid, and if he weeps I don't think, 'You're a man. You're not supposed to cry.'" They were able to support each other in a way that is impossible if a couple relies on artificial hope and cheerfulness all the time. This partnership continued after the babies were home and is a firm basis from which they cope with the household disruption and sheer hard work that twins inevitably entail.

But it is not, of course, only when things are difficult that a partner is needed. Many women write of the joy they experience when childbirth is shared, and say, "I could not have done it without him there." Many say that the partner's presence during labor and his emotional surrender at delivery is profoundly moving for them and that they will never forget this time. For the newly delivered woman it is not only the sight and feeling of the newborn lying on her body that is deeply moving, but what this means to her partner and his spontaneous emotional release into tears, laughter, and caresses. One man just said very slowly and clearly, "Wow . . . wooow . . . wooooow!" Not all fathers express themselves with dramatic abandon! Another, after having kissed his wife and telling her how clever she was, picked up the baby and danced around the room with her, singing "Waltzing Matilda." Some women say that although they did not have any strong sense that the baby belonged to them following delivery, when they saw the baby held in his father's arms and *his* response to his child, there was a rush of emotion and they promptly fell in love.

Sara and Philip decided to have their second baby at home. Philip describes it:

It is hard, impossible, to communicate to others the joy and wonder I experienced as my son slid out of Sara and with his mother's help onto her breast. Dan's tongue was belting away as if he had crawled into a desert oasis and was searching for the life-sustaining nectar.

Sara handed the baby to Philip as she delivered the placenta. "For the first time the reality of this life creation that Sara and I had shared for nine months was driven home . . . The birth of one's own child is," he says, "the happiest, most powerful experience a man can hope to witness." When the midwife had gone home they slept the rest of the night with their little daughter, too, all four together in the large bed. "She was curled against me," said Sara, "and Dan with Philip."

It seems that the intensity of such an experience for both parents prepares the way for powerful emotions that follow. Many couples say, "We are closer." One woman added, "In labor I learned to trust him absolutely. When Jake was born we were so deeply moved. Somehow that deepened our understanding of each other."

The birth is only one point in an emotional journey together that involves transformations in a couple's relationship as the child grows and as they discover new aspects of themselves. Sometimes these discoveries can be disconcerting, and the changes invariably produce fresh stresses as well as a new closeness, sharpening and further defining the elements of their partnership. One man, asked by his wife how he felt the birth of their daughter, now two years old, had affected their relationship, said, "It's strengthened the pluses of our marriage and deepened the minuses."

Birth need not be an isolated emotional "trip," although it is often reduced to that. It is part of a continuum in the relationship. Sharing in the birth of the child is a psychological experience of such significance that it gives an opportunity for two people to go on from there to evolve a richer life together as caring, sharing parents as well as lovers.

8

Coping with the Family

I got pregnant accidentally. When I told my sixteen-year-old I was pregnant, he said, "Hah! You talk to me about sex. But what about *you*? It's about time you started using condoms!"

It was awkward telling the children. Eventually, at about four and a half months, after getting them together one Saturday morning, my husband asked them to guess our news. They guessed we were divorcing, separating, going abroad, that he'd been fired, but none guessed correctly. They were amazed. The boys (twenty and eighteen) were easygoing and thought it was "a good idea," but Susan (fourteen) left the room and became very quiet. The next day she implied that it was thoughtless of us to let this happen. . . .

Many couples having a second family after a gap find the most difficult people to tell are their adolescent children. It is almost as if the open acknowledgment of sexual activity between parents compromises the young people in their own sexual identity. Boys may be horrified, and at this age they tend to be embarrassed by having a mother who looks pregnant. Girls say, "How *could* you, Mother!" as if she were discovered in some gross impropriety. One girl said to her father, "You *naughty* boy, Daddy!" and he was embarrassed in his turn. A boy of eleven exclaimed, "Oh, Mom, now you've gone and done it!" He would not touch his mother right through pregnancy or, at first, the baby. Another seemed concerned about his mother, but only, she suggests, because he wanted to be sure she could continue to cook his dinner!

One woman, who started a second family with a new partner, after a long gap, said, "Steven, at sixteen, was very much against the idea of a baby. He became anxious and depressed. He was articulate about his feelings: he said it made him feel that he and Joseph were just remnants of a failed marriage. He realized that the focus of the family would shift and that the boys would no longer be the center of attention. And both of them were worried that there would be less money—in particular that there wouldn't be enough to buy the clothes they wanted and their gym shoes!"

Ingrid says of her fourteen-year-old, "She worried about her friends' reactions to my appearance and her grades being impaired by 'a screaming baby.' " Another girl of this age "went through two very traumatic years and definitely resented the intrusion of noise, demands, toys, and diapers, and the time consumed by a baby. Whether her adolescent years would have been so difficult without the child, I don't know, but in suffering we grow as people and at nearly seventeen she has become well balanced," her mother says.

Loneliness

Even if their initial reactions are negative, older boys who have already gained some confidence in their own identity often seem to cope well with the experience. But this may take time. Steven, for example, stayed in bed for the whole first day after the birth and refused to look at the baby, though it was a home birth. His

I found it awkward to tell the children

mother said, "That was terribly painful. I wanted him to see the baby while he was brand new. He was in the next room, watching TV. The midwife went in and said, 'Come on, come and see the baby!' He resented that a lot—someone outside the family interfering. When I was up and about with the baby, he was averting his eyes every time we came near. Eventually I couldn't stand it any longer, and said, 'I've got needs, too, and this hurts me. I need your help!' I started giving him the baby to hold when I was busy. I didn't make a big deal out of it, and the barriers gradually slipped down. Now the baby is two, and he has come full circle. He decides he won't go out so that he can baby-sit, he carries him on his shoulders, and they go to the swings. He takes him out to meet his friends."

Girls under about the age of fourteen often identify unselfconsciously with their mothers in a very caring and compassionate way. A girl sometimes worries for her mother, too. One woman says that her daughter of twelve bought diapers out of her pocket money. Frances, a single mother who has just had another baby, says she did not realize how lonely her ten-year-old daughter had been:

> She was fantastically excited and got involved in my childbirth class—considering herself my partner, reading all the books. She was very good with the relaxation exercises. She cried when I lit a cigarette or had a drink, so I stopped. She was all the things supportive partners are supposed to be. Toward the end of the pregnancy she got very tense. We must have had the largest list of phone numbers and emergency procedures!

Anna feels that her pregnancy is a very good experience for her daughter of thirteen and says she has "shared" it:

> I have tried to keep her in touch with all my body changes and she has seen me naked. I feel it will be a help to her in the future to have absorbed all this, rather than come to it "cold" as I did.

However the information is received initially, most families seem to adjust not only well but with delight to a late addition. The eleven-year-old who would not touch his mother or the baby started playing with his sister in her first year, though roughly ("she loved it," his mother said), and is now "very tender and attached." Women say that a baby brings out a newfound tenderness in their sons and believe that it is a very positive preparation for later fatherhood. The "macho" typical of many male adolescents' picture of themselves gives way to gentleness and concern, and the whole family benefits. They no longer dash through the house with gangs of their friends, and even the stereos may be turned down. "Our family life has become softer and more caring," one woman says. A sixteen-year-old big brother changes his baby sister's diapers and is very gentle and playful with her. "He's mind-blowing," an eighteen-year-old says of his newborn brother; "Terrific," a sixteen-year-old says of a baby sister. An older brother of twenty remarks that he likes the changed form of the family now that it cuts right across the generations and, he feels, unites them all.

After she has adjusted to the idea, an adolescent daughter may become much closer to her mother in a shared womanhood, sometimes even in a kind of female conspiracy against men. One mother said of her daughter:

> She became more and more involved and helpful. She offered to stay with me for the birth, to be "a reliable help, unlike Daddy" as she put it.

It may be important for a girl to have time alone with her mother after the birth to discuss her often very conflicting feelings. While mother and baby are in the hospital, this is often impossible, and after their return home, there are so many visitors and such a lot of work that this time for quiet sharing can be crowded out. Elizabeth says her daughter developed a bad sore throat. They had a "good gossip" together the first time they were alone after the birth. Elly, who had been very excited about the baby coming and involved in all the details of the pregnancy, told her mother that she was worried that she did not love the baby immediately. Elizabeth said *she* felt just like that, too, and that it often took some time to get to know a baby.

Adolescents are good baby-sitters, although women say that they try not to take it for granted, and many make a regular arrangement to pay for time spent baby-sitting. A mother may find her son fixing his motorbike with the baby bouncing in her seat watching the fascinating proceedings. The younger child seems to benefit greatly from all this, though one mother says she is anxious that the baby, present "during the usual teenage arguments," may grow up undisciplined.

Being with older children provides an intellectual stimulus for the baby, but mothers describe ways in which they make sure that the younger child is able to meet children of about the same age, too. They notice how they themselves are enriched by contact with younger women and their children, opening a whole new social world that in the past they might not have thought they would enjoy, but that keeps them in touch with attitudes and concerns of couples still in their twenties.

Listening to Heartbeats

Children between four or five and early adolescence are rarely surprised by a pregnancy, and some have been urging their mothers to have a baby for years. For girls, friends at school who have younger babies at home to take care of are considered very special. The changes of pregnancy are followed with curiosity, and women say that this is a great educational opportunity for their older children. Both boys and girls can listen to the baby's heartbeat through a fetal stethoscope. If you know how your baby is lying, you may be able to locate the fetal heart yourself without difficulty in the last two or three months of pregnancy.

Lie back against pillows on a couch or bed and first feel with your hands where the most actively moving small knobs are placed at the moment. These are probably the feet and will often be at one side or the other right under your ribs. If the baby is active at the time, an older child can feel the kicks. Follow the legs around to the other side and you will reach the trunk; move down from there, about two hands' width, sliding your hand in a little as you do, and you reach the spot where it is probably easiest to hear the fetal heart. You will be at the level of your own navel or below. If the baby has engaged in your pelvis with its head down like an egg in an eggcup, this spot will be below your navel but out to the left or right side. Instead of a stethoscope you can use the cardboard cylinder from the middle of a toilet paper roll or a tumbler with the open end placed over the area where you hope to pick up sounds. When a baby is lying with her back against her mother's spine, the limbs are at the front of your abdomen, and it may be more difficult to detect the heartbeat because the limbs are in front of the chest. If your navel sinks in with a saucer-shaped depression in this area, this is probably the position your baby is in at the moment. If your navel sticks out with a rounded shape like a watermelon behind it, your baby is probably lying in the more usual anterior position and you will find it easier to pick up the heart. In the seventh and eighth months, babies change position frequently, often many times a day, so trying another time, when you feel the baby has shifted, may lead to success.

Women described the wonder their older children express when they hear the baby's heartbeats or are helped to locate the different parts of the baby and feel the movements. Most prenatal appointments take place during school hours, but some mothers take an older child along during her vacation so that she can understand what is happening and indirectly learn more about changes that may take place in her own body, too, in later years.

Some women choose to give birth at home partly because they feel that understanding about and sharing in birth can be important for the other children. The younger the other children, the more the mother is concerned about separation from them; the older they are, the more she sees the birth as a maturational experience for her sons and daughters.

Mary is forty and the older children are thirteen, eleven, and nine, a girl and two boys. She says she found that after having amniocentesis she got "hooked into the hospital system" regardless, but was unhappy about the conveyor belt atmosphere of the prenatal clinic and discovered that visiting by other siblings on postnatal wards was on weekends only. So she canceled her appointment and arranged a home birth, a really family-centered experience. When she was in the first stage of labor, "my eldest son came in and was a classic case of pacing up and down, saying, 'Are you all right?' The midwife chatted with him and he became much more relaxed." After the birth her daughter spent several hours just holding the baby. "She called her several times a 'dear little puppy,' and I remembered that a puppy was the only pet she'd had. The feelings about the two must have been similar."

Children can be invited to help with preparations for the new baby. This works best if they have some creative input and can use their own ideas. Sam, age five, has fabric paints and is painting giraffes, elephants, and rabbits on cotton shirts. (I wouldn't be surprised if there are some fighter planes, too.)

Changing Relationships

When the baby is born, new patterns of relationships in the family emerge. If a woman is preoccupied with her baby or feeling tired, older children tend to turn to their father more and also to become more self-reliant. This is very different from the more usual change in pattern when a newborn is introduced into a family where the older children are still under about five years. There, an older child, the displaced baby, may regress temporarily. A typical description of the mother of a two-year-old after the birth of a new baby:

> When Dinah came to visit me she had a good look at the baby and then got very whiny and noisy. My husband was suffering from a hangover so each bang and clatter made him wince. When we came home she would poke the baby through the bars of his crib "to see if he's awake." The poor child suffered from lack of sleep for a few weeks. When I was feeding Joe she would say she wanted a wee, so I would either have to have the potty chair in the room with me or try to get Dinah on the toilet with Joe hanging on to his means of nourishment for dear life.

With older children the mother often has the opposite impression: they grow up. She starts to see them through new eyes and is often astonished at the blossoming of qualities of caring and tenderness that she did not realize they possessed. One woman, commenting on the relationship of her three teenagers with their baby brother, says: "They have all been so positive and beautiful with him that this must be one of the biggest pluses of all." And a father, summing up the effect of the birth on the older children, aged twenty down to fourteen, says: "All seem to enjoy the change in structure that the baby has brought. Each child feels much more mature and responsible. . . . It has given the family a focus."

One disadvantage of having a baby later on, however, is that grandparents are not always alive, or well enough, to share in the joy of the new baby. Mothers see this as a sadness for them and a loss for the child. Some women feel torn between wanting to care for a sick parent and the child's needs as he or she grows and find it a great strain. Several women, however, described how a grandmother who was ill, or who had lost interest in life, gained a new sparkle with the birth of the baby. Some of these grandmothers had recently lost their husbands and were obviously still grieving painfully. The arrival of a baby helped them to come out of a sometimes prolonged mourning and had enormous psychological benefits for them.

A woman most appreciates her mother who lives near enough to offer regular practical help, rather than advice. As one says: "She has the baby for an hour at a time and allows me to recharge my batteries." It is sometimes possible to make friends with an older person in the neighborhood you can trust who can learn your ways and take over occasionally. An adopted grandmother or father provides a child with another loving adult, and the relationship brings great pleasure to an otherwise lonely older person.

Some grandmothers see the baby as a threat to them, depriving them of love they need from their son or daughter. The new mother then feels an extra drain on her strength as she tries to cope with the emotional demands of a lonely and unhappy parent as well as stresses of dealing with a family, new baby, and running a home. She may become very resentful of this parent, whether it is her own or her partner's mother, and it is important that the couple discuss their feelings together and develop a joint strategy to cope with the problem.

The birth of a child can profoundly affect the relationship of a woman with her own mother. This change may start in pregnancy. One woman, four months pregnant, says: "My parents have, at last, realized that I'm 'grown up' now and think twice before telling me what to do." Some women remain in an almost adolescent relationship with their mothers until they have their first baby. If this is not till they are after thirty, the bond between mother and daughter has become hard-set, the older woman treating her daughter as irresponsible, incompetent, and in need of protection, and the younger in a continual state of revolt.

Mothers

Part of the sense of freedom and of having matured that some women experience when they have a baby is that this relationship with their own mother undergoes rapid change. "We always had a terribly thorny relationship. All of a sudden I've become acceptable. I'm a mother—like her. At the same time, I understand the pressures she has been under as the mother of seven children." However concerned the older woman is that her daughter cannot take care of a baby properly, and even if she offers unwelcome advice in the first few months, after a while she usually begins to realize that she *can*. One woman said that recovering the happy relationship with her own mother, which she feels came with surrendering her defensiveness and learning to give love, brought deep satisfaction. "I am sure I was arrogant and selfish before. Loving a little baby is the completest joy."

When a woman already has a good relationship with her mother, the sharing between the two women further enriches it. Di said the fact that her mother had successfully breast-fed four of them helped develop her own confidence in breast-feeding. Her mother came to stay for a few weeks:

We've always been close, but for the first time I really understood the mother/child relationship. She never criticized anything I did, was interested in new ways of doing things, and was able to take my outbursts of temper (mainly due to tiredness) completely in her stride. She was my safety valve.

When sisters are emotionally close and noncompetitive, the new mother may find they can give her very good postnatal support. It is best not to have to get to know new people when you are most in need of an understanding friend to listen and give relaxed counseling and not be judgmental. Connie, whose two sisters gave her a great deal of support over the telephone, added that she also had a marvelous cleaning woman and a freezer full of cooked foods. These practical aspects of life can loom large after a baby comes. Some women, although they have sisters who have had babies, cannot happily use them to help during this period because they are still competing with them. Sometimes one element in actually having the baby is that a woman is locked in competition with a sister and wants to prove to her mother or father that she can do as well as her sister.

For most women, a mother-in-law, even a very understanding one, is classed as a "visitor" as compared with one's own mother. On the other hand, the birth of the baby may bring the new mother and her mother-in-law closer together. As one woman put it:

Because I was an academic, she didn't know how to treat me. I was "different." Now I've become "normal." Since the birth, my relationship with my mother-in-law has improved enormously. I did not feel any particular affinity with her for a long time, and she herself was probably thinking that I might not be good enough for HER SON! When she saw how well I was coping with the pregnancy, she already considered me better, but it was really on the day of the birth that the sudden change occurred. She was delighted with the baby, and in fact I think she was proud of me as well, as I did so well with the birth. And as her son thanked her for her giving birth to him as a baby ("Now I realize what *you* did!") she really blossomed into an even brighter smile, and her eyes were shining with the joy of being recognized, maybe for the first time in her life, and that by her son!

Sometimes a new mother knows already that she cannot cope with her mother-in-law for more than short periods at a time and that these have to be carefully planned in advance. If this is so, it is vital to discuss it with your husband so that he knows the strategy, realizes that you need his protection at this stage, and is not left feeling disloyal to both women. Connie, who got on so well with her own mother, was usually great friends with her husband's mother, too. But the two women could not agree about Connie's style of breast-feeding, and she knew that her mother-in-law was worried about prolonged breast-feeding and Dan getting interrupted sleep at nights. The baby was breast-fed whenever she wanted until she was sixteen months. At fifteen months she had a throat infection and rejected other foods, having fourteen feeds a day, not including those at night. "I know," said Connie, "because my mother-in-law, whom we were staying with and who was disgusted with the whole thing, had counted for me!" Once the infection cleared up, however, she weaned herself in four days. "That was one up on my mother-in-law, who is actually normally a very understanding person."

This is one of the bonuses of breast-feeding, that it is the perfect food if the child is ill, and may be not only the most comforting one but also the only one that she can digest and wants. In my own experience most of the crises in breast-feeding, when women seek help urgently, together with anxiety about not yet having weaned a child, come at times of the year when there are family gatherings and when members of the family go to stay with each other, such as Christmas and Easter or the summer holidays.

In some ways the older mother is immunized from the criticisms of those to whom she is nearest by her own experience of life. She knows that there is more than one way of doing things and that they probably all work. She is, as one woman put it, "less of a perfectionist and more of a human being," and is better able to relax and enjoy her baby than she would have been in her twenties.

9

Coping Alone

The woman alone faces special challenges in pregnancy, if only because she feels the whole burden of responsibility, for planning ahead, for supporting the child financially, for loving him, resting on her shoulders. A woman over thirty-five tends to take this on with understanding born from her experience of life, probably much more than someone still in her teens or twenties would.

For some women deciding to have a baby when they are in their thirties, the child is their "last chance" and conception is the consequence of a carefully thought-out decision that this is what they want. Some cannot find the right man with whom to form a partnership and are concerned only to have a child. Some do not wish to have a man anyway and prefer a loving relationship with another woman. A lesbian mother is usually not alone, and the relationship with her partner is often a good deal more stable than many heterosexual relationships. The woman who chooses artificial insemination has also taken time to work out what she wants, and the conception is far from the accident that it often is in a male-female partnership. Other women are having a child after a separation from the baby's father and occasionally after his death. The woman alone is, therefore, not one person but many, who may in fact have little in common with one another.

A woman who has no partner needs a good support network both before and after the baby comes. To start with, it is vital that she has a labor companion who goes with her to childbirth classes, works with her on breathing and relaxation, and understands exactly how to help in labor. To plan on having someone at the birth simply to hold your hand is not enough. You need someone really to share the labor and who has the skills to help you keep on an even course. This can be a woman friend, sister or other relative, childbirth educator or someone studying to be one, and I have known women who have had a trusted man friend take this on, too. A charming and sophisticated older man attended every single childbirth class in a course, on time even when his friend was late, accepting the responsibility because the father of her child was in his late teens and could not face it. He was present throughout the labor and delivery, experienced the rush of emotions that a new father usually does, and then had to stand back as the younger man decided that he liked the idea of being a father after all, now that the baby was safely born.

Birth Companions

One woman selected two lovers as birth companions. They were, according to the midwife, both "marvelous," and, she added, "I'm not sure which I would have chosen!" Another spent the major part of the first stage of labor with friends who lived near the hospital, a couple whom she had gotten to know in the childbirth class and whose own baby was three weeks old. The father of this baby had support techniques fresh in his mind, and had learned from his wife's experience, so he shepherded her through to eight centimeters dilation with masterly skill.

The important thing is that the single woman has someone with her whose task it is to concentrate on her needs as a person, not a reproductive body, and whose responsibilities are not divided between this relationship and medical tasks. This is why it is not enough to rely on a midwife for this, however kind and caring she is.

Still in some hospitals a woman may be left alone in labor. Still when wards are full, drugs may be used by busy staff members in place of personal help and understanding. Pat says she went into the hospital far too early, probably because she was alone and felt she would not be able to cope by herself if she waited until contractions were coming five minutes apart:

> The contractions stopped for about twelve hours, but it was nice because they weren't busy and the nurses all talked about how I was going to manage on my own and seemed genuinely interested. Unfortunately, Andrew decided to be born at their busy time, and the entirely unsympathetic night staff had taken over. I was totally out of control, couldn't do any of the exercises I'd practiced so assiduously, and felt like a complete coward. In the end, they gave me an injection and put me out.

An alternative arrangement is for this companion to be with you at home, rather than only turning up at the hospital, so that you can spend early labor in familiar surroundings. It helps to get into the rhythm of breathing and relaxing in the first half of the first stage in a close partnership, without the intrusion of other people if this can be avoided. Susan, whose lover was abroad and whom she did not want to involve any more than he wished, because she had not consulted him about starting the pregnancy, says that no one can ever talk to her of independence who has not made the journey alone to a hospital to have a baby, and then, three days later, come out of it, going down to the parking lot, picking up the baby at the maternity entrance, and driving off.

A birth companion should have the knowledge to be able to be a "patient advocate," if necessary. A woman in labor needs to be able to rely on someone to say if she is in the middle of a contraction and does not wish to have an injection of narcotics; to remind her that she should be given a vaginal examination immediately before having an epidural just in case she is already almost fully dilated; perhaps to say, before an episiotomy (a surgical cut to enlarge the birth opening) is done, that her friend did hope she might be able to manage without one and would it be possible to see if "breathing the baby out" would help. A patient advocate cannot, by definition, be an employee of a hospital. Anybody working for the hospital is bound to have divided loyalties. To say this may be hurtful to a nurse who sees her role as being on her patient's side, but as Norma Swenson of the Boston Women's Health Collective points out, though attractive as a concept, an alliance between consumers and professionals is unrealistic because the woman having a baby has transient and unequal status in the hospital system.[1]

Often a birth companion can attend at least some of your prenatal appointments, too, and look around the maternity unit in advance. Someone unfamiliar with hospitals may find this especially helpful. One woman, reluctant about getting fully involved with her partner's birth, felt much more relaxed about this after meeting the staff and finding them friendly. She said she now began to see her role more clearly and would not feel out of place.

Powerful Emotions

With other partners, just as with husbands, powerful emotions are often involved, and it is a mistake to think that a companion is there simply to remind you of exercises or rub your back. One man, married with two small children, who had been present at the births of both of them, supported his mistress through a pregnancy with his child, doing so because he felt it was right, but unwilling to break up his marriage. Duty, responsibility, compassion, whatever he felt, gave way to a passionate outpouring of emotion as he relived the births of his other children. He expressed his pain and joy, and in some inexplicable way this assurance of his emotional surrender to the experience gave the woman who was bearing his child great psychological support.

Another, attending classes with her lesbian partner, had herself had a pregnancy the previous year, which had finished in a late miscarriage. It must have been stressful for her to allow herself to identify completely with the woman having the baby and give herself completely to her in loving support, but she did so.

Sometimes the choice of support partner is a woman's own mother. It is vitally important for the mother to share preparation with her daughter if she is to be with her in labor. Not only have birth styles changed, with apparatus in the delivery room that the mother may not have seen before, but women tend to bring their own experiences of childbearing with them into the birth they attend. If these were unhappy, a mother may not be able to help her daughter gain confidence.

Faith's mother was deeply distressed to learn that her daughter was pregnant. She prayed that she be saved from sin every day. She did not know what to do, whether to turn Faith away or look forward to the birth of the baby with her. She spoke to the pastor at the Evangelical church she attended, who suggested that the right thing was to give her daughter her unconditional love. Faith was very happy with her mother's changed attitude, and at my suggestion asked her if she would come to childbirth classes with her. She said she had always been very inhibited about anything to do with sex and she did not know how her mother would take all the talk about bodies and feelings. Her labor had been a terrible and frightening ordeal. She had never had another baby because of what she had suffered with Faith. In any event, Faith need not have worried. Her mother, brought up in ignorance of her body, was hungry for information and obviously enjoyed the group, asked questions, discussed vigorously with the other couples present, and told me that her life would have been so different if she had known all this earlier and had been able to see it for the miracle it was. She supported her daughter magnificently through a drug-free labor, and the two became friends as never before.

The role of the support person can, perhaps, best be illustrated by describing the way a particular partnership worked during a painful induced labor in which a cesarean section was always in the cards and a forceps delivery very likely. The support that this single mother had from another woman gave her the confidence, courage, and trust in her body which resulted in a spontaneous birth.

Felicia had been warned that she would probably need a cesarean section. She was having a big baby and was of small build. Jo, her friend, had a baby daughter herself. She came to childbirth classes with Felicia, determined to give her full support through what was an emotionally difficult time, not only because of the uncertainty about the birth, but because Felicia was beginning to realize that the father of her baby was not going to leave his wife and children and was very anxious that it might leak out that he had fathered a baby outside the marriage. Both women kept careful notes during as much of the labor as they could and recorded the rest immediately afterward.

Jo's Diary

Jo's diary starts when the midwife called from the hospital to say that the induction had started and Felicia was asking for her:

> Packed ice into thermos and shot off in taxi. Did relaxing exercises myself in taxi so would bring a calm, reassuring atmosphere with me.

Once there, the first thing she had to do was to work out the best place to stand in the labor room, which was equipped spaceship style. She needed to be out of the midwife's way, not obstructing the equipment, yet close enough to Felicia to touch and hold her when she seemed to want this. She could see from the clock that each contraction was lasting about forty-five seconds.

> . . . but I felt that the best thing for me to do was to watch Felicia and try to see what she wanted. I talked to her between contractions, making her laugh a bit because I felt that was what

she needed, and keeping silent with just my hand on her arm during contractions, watching her face and hands and feet to see if they were tensing up, and occasionally just lightly stroking her shoulder for reassurance and to check that it was relaxed. In between contractions I checked that the thermos with ice was nearby and washcloths and lip salve.

I made a point of asking everyone who came in for any length of time what their name was, as I felt that the more personal the process was, the more confident Felicia would be, and once somebody has given you their name there is less tendency to be high-handed.

After about one and a half hours, contractions were stronger,

. . . and from now on I didn't move away from her at all. . . . If I moved from one side to let the nurses get at the equipment I moved to the other or held her feet very gently until I could put my hand on her upper arm, which was where she seemed to prefer it.

The machine monitoring the contractions and the baby's heart-beat was not functioning too well, so there was quite a lot of coming and going and tinkering about, which Felicia found distracting. So every time it happened, I told her quietly not to take any notice of them, they weren't important (which must have gone over well with the staff if they heard).

Somebody came to deal with the monitor, whom Jo asked firmly but politely to keep his voice down:

He seemed surprised and obviously thought it rather funny. Then a staff nurse told Felicia to turn over and started to move her mid-contraction. I said quietly, so as not to disturb Felicia, "Could you wait until this contraction is over?" She said, "But she has to turn on her side." I said, "Yes, but not now. Could it wait a minute? Then she could help you herself." It must have carried force because although she looked daggers at me, she waited until I said, "OK," and then we got Felicia over and tried to make her as comfy as possible.

After another two and a quarter hours, Felicia said she could not bear any more and she would like some pain medication, but as soon as she had had the injection she started to feel desperate and said she wanted an epidural:

> I told her the medication took a quarter of an hour to work, that although it must seem like forever, did she want to try and ride out the quarter hour? I promised I would tell her when it was up. I said that if she didn't want to wait I'd get someone to do the epidural. She said she would wait and between contractions I told her the time and how much longer there was to go till the end of the quarter hour. I could see the medication had started to work and I told her and when she said that she was OK told her how well she was doing and how wonderfully she had got through that quarter hour.

Felicia says: "I coped only with Jo. Without her I might have gone under." This is how she describes the help Jo gave her:

> She was encouraging me all the time, saying "relax into it— you're doing very well—very good," and praising and encouraging me. Throughout, a battery of doctors and nurses kept coming in, and the monitoring equipment kept going wrong.

The clip on the baby's head was not registering the fetal heart, so another monitor was strapped around her abdomen.

> After five hours I was beginning to tire of riding the pain. Jo said, "Don't worry about the other people, just breathe, keep breathing, you're doing well, you've made it, well done!" . . . At the point where I was tiring a nurse did a vaginal exam and I was only five to six centimeters dilated! I thought another five hours of this is impossible, but Jo said to me, "You know it goes much quicker from now on."

Felicia said it was a "marathon." She kept asking Jo for water, who put a small sponge soaked in icy water from the thermos in her mouth to suck. Her mouth became very dry because when she reached the end of the first stage most of her breathing was done through her mouth. Sometimes Jo could hardly get to the flask before another contraction came. "She also wiped my face with a warm washcloth. I especially liked to feel that on my cheeks and her warm hand on my arm through the contractions."

At last she began to want to push, and here Jo takes over again:

I kept gently tipping her head down so that her chin was tucked in as she tended to throw her head back. There seemed to be no progress and the doctor came in ready to do a forceps delivery. Then as they got her feet into the stirrups the baby's head rounded the corner and Felicia said she could feel it. Someone looked and said, "I can see the top of the head." I said to Felicia, "You're going to do it yourself after all." The doctor said, "I think I'm going to see a normal birth. I haven't seen one for years. See if you can break my run." I dashed down to see and saw a little dark mass and rushed up and told her I could see the baby's head.

Felicia pushed; the baby slid out and was given to her to hold immediately.

Black tendrils of hair damp from the uterus, cheeks like a ripe peach, and huge eyes, violet-blue, looking straight up to her. She was plump and firm and amazingly hot, straight from a tropical uterine climate. The mother was laughing and crying at the same time. She drew the baby closer, holding her hungrily, devouring with her eyes the reality of this little person who stared at her quite calmly, as if to say: "So this is my mother!" Jo was crying, too. Her arm was around Felicia as she held the child. Their closeness was like petals touching, overlapping, folded in and curving over the baby.

A Chance to Grow

The birth of a child can be, and is for many women, an opening up of the new, an unfolding of love, not only for the baby, but perhaps for those from whom we have been guarding and protecting ourselves, and a step on the journey toward deeper understanding of ourselves and others. We can never possess our children. But through them, and with their help, we have a chance to grow as human beings.

Notes

Chapter 2: Planning Ahead for Pregnancy

1. "Masculinization of the female fetus due to use of orally given progesterone," L. Wilkins, *Journal of American Medical Association* 172: 1028–32, 1960.
2. "Birth defects and oestrogen and progesterone in pregnancy," S. Harlap et al., *The Lancet* 1: 692–93, 1975; "Epidemiological problems associated with studies of the safety of oral contraceptives," D. Seigal and P. Corfman, *Journal of American Medical Association* 203: 950, 1968; "Oral contraception: potential hazards of hormone therapy during pregnancy," J. Robertson-Rintoul, *The Lancet* 2: 1315, 1974.
3. *Women and the Crisis in Sex Hormones,* B. and G. Seaman, Bantam, New York, 1978.
4. "Factors governing IUD performance," R. P. Bernard, *American Journal of Public Health* 61: 559–67, 1971.
5. *Epidemiology and Community Health* 45: 159–63, 1991.
6. "Cigarette smoking in pregnancy and fetal hyperviscosity." Peter C. Buchan, *British Medical Journal* 286: 1315, 1983.
7. "Maternal smoking and childhood asthma," M. Weitzman, S. Gortmaker, D. Klein Walker, and A. Sobol, *Pediatrics* 85, 4: 505–11, 1990.
8. Mark Bulterys, Sander Greenland, and Jess Kraus, *Pediatrics* 86:

535–40, 1990; reported in *Journal of American Medical Association* 264: 21, 2731, 1990; "Sudden infant death syndrome and maternal smoking," Michael H. Malloy, Howard J. Hoffman, and Donald R. Peterson, *American Journal of Public Health* 82: 10, 1381, 1990.

9. "Maternal smoking and accelerated placental maturation," Michael G. Pinette, Kimberly Loftus-Brault, Deborah A. Nardi, and John F. Rodis, *Obstetrics and Gynecology* 73, 3, part 1: 379–82, 1989.

10. "Association of interauterine cigarette smoke exposure with indices of fetal lung maturation," E. Lieberman, J. Torday, R. Barbiere, A. Cohen, H. Van Vunakis, and S. T. Weiss, *Obstetrics and Gynecology* 79, 4: 564–70, 1992.

11. "Smoking during pregnancy," B. B. K. Pirani, *Obstet. Gynecol: Survey* 33, 1, 1–13, 1978; *Smoking and Health. A Report of the Surgeon General* (U.S. Department of Health, Education and Welfare, 1979), Chapter 8; "Cigarette smoking in pregnancy." Leader in *British Medical Journal*, 28 August 1976.

12. "The fetal alcohol syndrome," *Drug Abuse and Alcoholism Newsletter II:* 4 May 1978.

13. "Alcohol and advice to the pregnant woman," Griffith Edwards, *British Medical Journal* 286: 247, 1983.

14. "Prevention of preeclampsia with low-dose aspirin in healthy nulliparous pregnant women," Baha Sibai et al., *New England Journal of Medicine* 329, 17: 1213–18 and 1265–66, 1993.

15. Adapted from *Obstetrics*, Gordon Stirrat, Grant McIntyre, London, 1981.

16. "Hyperthermia as a possible teratogenic agent," David W. Smith et al., *Journal of Pediatrics* 92: 6, 878–83, June 1978; "Maternal hyperthermia as a possible cause of anencephaly," Peter Miller et al., *Lancet* I: 8063, 519–21, 1978.

17. "How does strenuous maternal exercise affect the fetus?" Susan L. Woodward, *Birth and the Family Journal* 8: I, 1981.

Chapter 3: Will the Baby Be All Right?

1. "Prenatal screening for Down's syndrome," R. Keatinge and E. S. Williams, *British Medical Journal* 303: 54–55, 1991.

2. "Miracles in the womb," Wendy Varley, *Parents*, April 1989, 56–59.

3. "Ignorance meant we nearly lost Harry," Carol Taylor, *The Independent*, 17 December 1991.

4. "Estimated rates of clinically significant cytogenetic abnormality (other than Down's syndrome) by one-year maternal age intervals," E. B. Hook and D. K. Cross, *American Journal of Human Genetics* 31: 136a, 1979.

5. "Does routine ultrasound scanning improve outcome in pregnancy? Metaanalysis of various outcome measures," H. C. Bucher, J. G. Schmidt, *British Medical Journal* 307: 13–17, 1993. "Ultrasound screening perinatal mortality: controlled trial of systematic one-stage screening in pregnancy," A. Saari-Kemppainen et al., The Helsinki Ultrasound Trial, *Lancet* 336: 387–91, 1990.

6. "I felt I was killing my baby . . . while my instincts were to protect it," Kay Marles, *Good Housekeeping*, September 1990.

7. "Serum screening for Down's syndrome: some women's experiences," H. Statham and J. Green, *British Medical Journal* 307: 174–76, 1993.

8. "Screening for fetal abnormalities: attitudes and experiences," J. Green, H. Statham, and C. Snowdon, in T. Chard, M. P. M. Richards (eds.), *Obstetrics in the 1990s: Current Controversies, Clinics in Developmental Medicine*, KacKeith Press, London, 1992, 123–24.

9. Kay Marles, op. cit.

10. "Chorionic villus sampling," T. W. Meade and A. Grant, *British Medical Journal* 304: 185–86, 1992.

11. H. Statham and G. Green, op. cit.

12. "Use of cordocentesis in fetal hemolytic disease and autoimmune thrombocytopenia," C. P. Weiner, *American Journal of Obstetrics and Gynecology* 162: 1126–27, 1990.

13. SAFTA, Soho Square, London WIV 6JB, 29–30.

14. "Professional understanding and parent's experience of termination," H. Statham, in D. J. H. Brock et al., *Prenatal Diagnosis and Screening*, Churchill Livingstone, London, 1992.

Chapter 4: Prenatal Care

1. *An Interesting Condition: The Diary of a Pregnant Woman*, Abigail Lewis, Odhams, London, 1951.

2. "Twenty-four-hour studies of fetal respiratory movements and fetal body movements in normal and abnormal pregnancies," A. Roberts et al., *The Current Status of Fetal Heart Rate Monitoring and Ultrasound in Obstetrics* 209–20, R.C.O.G, London, 1977.

3. A. M. Grant, D. Elbourne, L. Valentine, S. Alexander, "Routine formal fetal movement counting and risk of antepartum late death in normally formed singletons," *Lancet* 2: 345–49, 1989.

Chapter 5: Doctors

1. *Men Who Control Women's Health,* Diana Scully, Houghton Mifflin, Boston, 1980.

2. *Subject Women,* Ann Oakley, Robertson, Oxford, 1981.

3. P. S. Byrne and P. E. L. Long, *Doctors Talking to Patients,* HMSO, London, 1976.

4. Harold Francis, "Obstetrics: a consumer oriented service? The case against," *Maternal and Child Health* 10: 3, 69, 1985.

5. "Late-bloomers: giving birth after thirty-five," *The Birth Gazette* 3: 1, 16–17, 1986.

6. "Care during the second stage of labor," J. Sleep et al., *Effective Care in Pregnancy and Childbirth,* vol. 2, Oxford University Press, New York, 1989; "Midline episiotomies—more harm than good," P. Shione et al., *Obstetrics and Gynecology* 75: 765–70, 1990; "Does episiotomy prevent perineal trauma and pelvic floor relaxation," M. C. Klein et al., *Online Journals of Current Clinical Trials,* 1 July 1992 (doc. #10).

7. *Some Women's Experiences of Induction,* Sheila Kitzinger, National Childbirth Trust, London, 2d ed., 1978.

8. *Maternal-Infant Bonding,* Marshall Klaus and John Kennell, Mosby, St. Louis, 1976.

9. *Practical Obstetric Problems,* Ian Donald, Lloyd-Luke, London, 1979. Harper & Row, New York, 5th ed., 1979.

10. Donald, ibid.

11. "The changing epidemiology of mortality and morbidity in mothers and babies in recent years." Paper presented at a Study Group on Problems in Obstetrics organized by the Medical Information Unit of the Spastics Society. Tunbridge Wells, April 1975; "Induction of labour and perinatal mortality," R. H. Tipton and B. V. Lewis, *British Medical Journal* 1: 361, 1975.

12. Donald, op. cit.

13. "Induction and acceleration of labor in modern obstetric practice." Paper presented at a Study Group on Problems in Obstetrics organized by the Medical Information Unit of the Spastics Society. Tunbridge Wells, April 1975.

14. See *Birth Rites, Birth Rights,* Judith Lumley and Jill Astbury, Sphere, Australia, 1980.
15. "Antecedents of handicap," Ross G. Mitchell, *Lancet II* 821: 86–87, 1981.

Chapter 6: Life After the Baby Comes

1. In *Winter Trees,* Sylvia Plath, Faber, London, 1972. Harper & Row, New York, 1972.
2. *The Edible Woman,* Margaret Atwood, Virago, London, 1980. Warner Books, New York, 1983.
3. *Maternal Infant Bonding,* Marshall Klaus and John Kennell, Mosby, St. Louis, 1976.
4. "Helping mothers to love their babies," *British Medical Journal* 2: 595, 1977.

Chapter 7: Partners

1. *Maternal Care and Mental Health,* John Bowlby, London, World Health Organization, 1951; *Child Care and the Growth of Love,* John Bowlby, Penguin, London, 1953; *Attachment,* John Bowlby, Penguin, London, 1971. Basic Books, New York, 1969.
2. "The development of social attachments in infancy," H.R. Schaffer and P. E. Emerson, *Monographs of Social Research in Child Development* 29: 3, 1–77, 1964.
3. *A World of Women,* Erica Bourguignon, Praeger, New York, 1980.
4. *The Speaking Tree: A Study of Indian Culture and Society,* Richard Lannoy, Oxford University Press, New York, 1971.
5. Sheila Kitzinger, unpublished research in Jamaica; *Women as Mothers,* Sheila Kitzinger, Fontana, 1978. Random House, New York, 1979.
6. "Depressive illness in general practice," A. M. W. Porter, *British Medical Journal* 28 March, 773–78, 1970.
7. *Feminine Personality and Conflict,* J. M. Bardwick et al., Wadsworth, Belmont, California, 1970.
8. *Subject Women,* Ann Oakley, Robertson, Oxford, 1981. Pantheon, New York, 1981.
9. *Biorhythms and Human Reproduction,* ed. Michel Ferin et al., Wiley, New York, 1984.
10. *Biological Rhythms in Psychiatry and Medicine,* G. G. Luce, U.S.P.H.C. 2088, U.S. Dept. of Health, Washington, D.C., 1970.

11. Ferin et al., op. cit.

12. "Emotional cycles in man," R. B. Hersey, *Journal of Mental Science* 77: 151–69, 1931.

13. Luce, op. cit.

14. *Sex Differences in Behavior,* H. Persky, in R. C. Friedman et al., Wiley, New York, 1978.

15. *Parent-Infant Bonding,* Marshall H. Klaus and John H. Kennell, Mosby, St. Louis, 2d ed., 1982.

Chapter 9: Coping Alone

1. *Maternity Care in Ferment,* Maternity Center Association, New York, 1980.

Index